Sunday Matters

Dominican Series

The Dominican Series is a joint project by Australian Dominican women and men and offers contributions on topics of Dominican interest and various aspects of church, theology and religion in the world.

Series Editors: Mark O'Brien OP and Gabrielle Kelly OP

1. *English for Theology: A Resource for Teachers and Students*, Gabrielle Kelly OP, 2004.
2. *Towards the Intelligent Use of Liberty: Dominican Approaches in Education*, edited by Gabrielle Kelly OP and Kevin Saunders OP, 2007.
3. *Preaching Justice: Dominican Contributions to Social Ethics in the Twentieth Century*, edited by Francesco Campagnoni OP and Helen Alford OP, 2008.
4. *Don't Put Out the Burning Bush: Worship and Preaching in a Complex World*, edited by Vivian Boland OP, 2008.
5. *Bible Dictionary: Selected Biblical and Theological Words*, Gabrielle Kelly OP in collaboration with Joy Sandefur, 2008.

Disclaimer:
Views expressed in publications within the Dominican Series do not necessarily reflect those of the respective Congregations of the Sisters or the Province of the Friars.

Sunday Matters

Reflections on the Lectionary Readings for Year A

Mark A O'Brien OP

2010

Text copyright © 2010 remains with the author.

All rights reserved. Except for any fair dealing permitted under the Copyright Act, no part of this book may be reproduced by any means without prior permission. Inquiries should be made to the publisher.

National Library of Australia Cataloguing-in-Publication entry (pbk)

Author: O'Brien, Mark A., 1945-
Title: Sunday matters : reflections on the lectionary readings year A / Mark O'Brien.
ISBN: 9781921817007 (pbk.)
Series: Dominican series ; 6
Notes: Includes index.
Subjects: Bible--Homiletical use.
Lectionary preaching--Catholic Church.

Dewey Number: 269.2

Cover design by Astrid Sengkey
Original artwork by Yvonne Ashby
Original lino cut by Yvonne Ashby

An imprint of the ATF Ltd
PO Box 504
Hindmarsh, SA 5007
ABN 90 116 359 963
www.atfpress.com

Table of Contents

Introduction	1
Introduction to the Gospel of Matthew	7
First Sunday of Advent	9
Second Sunday of Advent	11
Third Sunday of Advent	13
Fourth Sunday of Advent	15
Christmas (Midnight)	17
Christmas	19
Holy Family	23
Mary Mother of God	25
The Epiphany	27
Baptism of the Lord	29
First Sunday of Lent	31
Second Sunday of Lent	35
Third Sunday of Lent	39
Fourth Sunday of Lent	41
Fifth Sunday of Lent	43
Palm Sunday of the Passion	45
Thursday in Holy Week	49

Good Friday	51
Easter	55
Second Sunday of Easter	59
Third Sunday of Easter	61
Fourth Sunday of Easter	63
Fifth Sunday of Easter	67
Sixth Sunday of Easter	71
Ascension of the Lord	73
Pentecost	75
Trinity Sunday	79
Body and Blood of Christ (*Corpus Christi*)	81
Second Sunday of the Year	83
Third Sunday of the Year	85
Fourth Sunday of the Year	87
Fifth Sunday of the Year	91
Sixth Sunday of the Year	93
Seventh Sunday of the Year	95
Eighth Sunday of the Year	97
Ninth Sunday of the Year	99
Tenth Sunday of the Year	101
Eleventh Sunday of the Year	103
Twelfth Sunday of the Year	105
Thirteenth Sunday of the Year	109
Fourteenth Sunday of the Year	111
Fifteenth Sunday of the Year	113
Sixteenth Sunday of the Year	117
Seventeenth Sunday of the Year	119
Eighteenth Sunday of the Year	123

Nineteenth Sunday of the Year	125
Twentieth Sunday of the Year	127
Twenty First Sunday of the Year	129
Twenty Second Sunday of the Year	131
Twenty Third Sunday of the Year	133
Twenty Fourth Sunday of the Year	135
Twenty Fifth Sunday of the Year	139
Twenty Sixth Sunday of the Year	143
Twenty Seventh Sunday of the Year	147
Twenty Eighth Sunday of the Year	151
Twenty Ninth Sunday of the Year	153
Thirtieth Sunday of the Year	155
Thirty First Sunday of the Year	159
Thirty Second Sunday of the Year	163
Thirty Third Sunday of the Year	165
Our Lord Jesus Christ, Universal King	169
Extras For Year A	**173**
Year 2014 Presentation of the Lord	175
Ss Peter and Paul, Apostles	177
Triumph of the Holy Cross	179
Commemoration of all the Faithful Departed	181
Dedication of the Lateran Basilica	185
Year 2017 Transfiguration	187
Suggested Readings	**191**
Biblical Index	**193**
Subject Index	**199**

Introduction

Sunday matters or should matter to Christians. It is the Lord's day and so the most important day of the week, a time for us to acknowledge God as the source, centre and goal of our lives. Because Sunday is a matter of importance there are important matters to consider on this day, such as time for prayer, worship and being nourished by the Word of God. Sunday also matters because it is a limited amount of time and these days there are a host of other things competing for our time and attention: sport, shopping, TV, travel, etc. Deciding what to do on Sundays and other major days of the Christian calendar has become something of a challenge for contemporary Christians, some would say even a crisis.

But a crisis or a challenge can provide an opportunity to rethink and refocus. The reflections on the lectionary readings for Sundays and major feasts are designed to show that the Bible itself is an invitation or challenge to think. It does not impose its views because that would be most ungodlike—according to the biblical understanding of God. Much of life is about making decisions and the Bible challenges us to decide where our priorities lie. The reflections offered are relatively short (around eight hundred words each) so that all the Sundays and major feasts of a liturgical year can be included in one book. This volume covers year A of the Roman Catholic Lectionary; subsequent volumes will cover years B and C. This also meant that not every reading could be given equal attention.

These reflections originally appeared in the *Australasian Catholic Record* over a three year period as 'Reflections on the Readings of Sundays and Feasts' (2007—9).[1] Although not homilies they were composed with

---

1. I am grateful to Dr Gerard Kelly, President of the Catholic Institute of Sydney and editor of ACR, for inviting me to do the reflections.

homiletic preparation in mind. In the light of readers' comments and further reflection, some have been revised, others rewritten and new ones added in order to cover all the Sundays of the three-year cycle and make the material more accessible to the general reader as well as the preacher. Those who do not have a lectionary or follow its cycle of readings can easily correlate biblical text and reflection by consulting the index at the back of the book.

It may be of help to readers to outline briefly some of the major ways in which the Bible has been read over the centuries and some of the major themes that I judge the Bible addresses. A good starting point is the recognition that we all communicate by expressing something in a certain way or form and within a certain context. In the Hebrew Bible/Old Testament the preferred literary forms are narrative (story, report, genealogy, etc), poetry (psalms, proverbs, prophecies) and law (commands, prohibitions, instructions); in the New Testament they are narrative (in the gospels and Acts of the Apostles) and letters (of Paul and others). A literary form provides a creative opportunity yet imposes limitations. For example, a story usually involves a plot (such as overcoming an evil) with a limited cast of characters. A storyteller has to develop the plot towards some form of resolution and this means being selective, otherwise the story could become too unwieldy and lose something of its impact.

What authors include in or leave out of their compositions is also influenced by their historical and social context. The context in which ancient authors operated had no equivalent to the modern novel with its intricate plots, large cast of characters and elaborate detail—but even these have their limitations. Most biblical stories or parables, songs or prophecies, are fairly short and it is likely much of what we have in the Bible are written 'distillations' of longer oral performances.[2] Writing in ancient times was time consuming and expensive: it is unlikely a scribe could write down all of an actual performance. To my mind they were very adept at recording the outline of a story or song, the key elements that would guide further performances. Stories, poems, gospels and letters were written for public proclamation, elaboration and comment. Thankfully, this is still the case for our Sunday liturgies in which a short selection of texts from the Bible is proclaimed for us to listen to, to preach on and to discuss. People in ancient times had excellent memories but they also had a smaller corpus of material to memorise. We now have to rely on computers and memory

---

2. On storytelling for example, see Antony F Campbell 'The Storyteller's Role: Reported Story and Biblical Text', *Catholic Biblical Quarterly* 64 (2002) 427-41.

sticks to store an ever increasing corpus of texts that is beyond our capacity to memorise.

I have been trained in modern western critical methods of reading the Bible but I also respect the traditional ways of reading that have been used in the church and synagogue since their inception. Both have to operate with the fundamental premise that one can only understand what a text is communicating by paying close attention to the way it is communicating (in story, poem or letter form). We all do this instinctively with literature with which we are familiar: we distinguish headline from commentary, editorial from a letter to the editor, advertisement from operating manual. Sporting enthusiasts know that a headline announcing 'cats maul dogs' is about a football match not a brawl between pets. When we come to the literature of another culture we need to be aware that two different contexts are coming in contact—our own and that of the other culture.

One could say that the traditional way of reading the Bible in the church assumed a close relationship between the biblical text, its inspired author or authors, and readers. When one read the book of Isaiah, for example, one heard the words of the prophet and through his words, the Word of God. One's faith context was also seen as important. Christians believed that reading Isaiah within the context of their faith enabled them to see the deeper, Christian, meaning of the book. Inspired New Testament authors operated in this context and the church and its theologians sought to follow their lead.

But contexts can change, and the Renaissance and Enlightenment periods in Europe led to a heightened awareness of the difference between the 'present world' and the ancient or classical world. One needed to reconstruct its context and ways of communicating in order to understand it. This in turn led many to the conviction that layers of interpretation over the centuries had obscured the original, real, meaning of the Bible, particularly the Hebrew Bible/Old Testament. The new critical analysis set out to recover the original meaning of each book of the Bible and through this the thinking of each author. Paradoxically however, this analysis concluded that many books of the Bible had multiple authors and editors and had undergone a long gestation. One could no longer be sure which parts of Isaiah came from Isaiah and which from later editors or scribes. Historical critical analysis opened up the world of the Bible to the reader and showed how divine inspiration can embrace all phases of a text's production, from the spirit filled prophet, to the community that preserves his or her preaching, to the careful work of a later scribe. But a clear connection between text and purported author could no longer be assured and critics of the approach accused it of fragmenting the Bible, assigning bits of texts to different authors and editors. Others shifted their attention to analysing biblical books as literary works of art, irrespective of who the author, authors or editors might have been.

The context of readers has changed again more recently with the rise of psychological and social sciences. This development has shifted the focus of attention from the author to the reader, what some call the 'subjective factor'. A lot of energy is now expended studying the dynamic relationship between a text and reader. In a sense this is a positive move because in the end it is the reader who has to say what he or she thinks a text means. The danger of course is that one can replace authorial intention with reader's invention. To try and prevent this, critical analysis insists that one must pay attention to the way the various parts of the text have been arranged—presumably by one or more authors. Even though the traditional relationship between author, text and reader has been pulled apart and dissected by critical analysis, there is now broad agreement that we need to keep their relationship in mind, even though we will probably never get the balance quite right. We are only human beings after all. Wrestling with such issues is part of the adventure of reading and discussing the Bible, or any text for that matter. We can learn from different perspectives, differing contexts.

It is a risky business to try and identify key theological themes in the rich and varied books that make up the Bible but life is about risks so here is an attempt. A key theme is love; primarily God's unconditional love of us and, as a result of this, our love of God, neighbour and ourselves. God hates the evil we do but loves us despite our evildoing. The biblical meaning of love emphasises loyalty and commitment. According to the Bible's claim, Israel is the chosen people to mediate God's love to the world; according to Christian faith, this divine love is most intensely and perfectly enshrined in the figure of Jesus. How is God's love revealed? Primarily, so the Bible claims, through justice and mercy/kindness. It is important to remember that the Bible explores these key terms within a context of injustice and cruelty. Augustine once said: 'love and do what you will'. If we really did love we would will to do what the lover (God) wants. But because we are flawed and sinful creatures we need to learn to love by being just and merciful. A theology of God as just means that God is intolerant of evil and acts to remove it and establish a just society or world. But God's justice is always kind and merciful, what is best for humanity. To use another biblical term, it is about salvation.

The great challenge for biblical people, as for ourselves, was to assess their experience/history in relation to justice and mercy, both on the individual, national an international scale (God is Lord of all history). Prophets intervened at times to challenge Israel about its conduct and proclaim that God would punish it for its infidelity to the covenant established at Sinai (book of Exodus). If prophets did not proclaim this message the theology of a just and merciful God would lose its authority. Punishment did not mean the covenant relationship was ended. God remained committed to Israel and would in due course restore it to the land and enable it to live as a just society, a beacon for all the nations of the world. This is a broad theological schema that makes a faith claim, it cannot be proved nor does it try to answer all the particular issues and questions that arise for each individual or each generation. This is not the Bible's purpose. Rather, it offers a 'big picture' or framework within which we are challenged to make decisions about our lives.

Christians believe that Jesus is the one sent by God, the only Son, to fulfil Israel's mission to the world. He showed his complete and unconditional commitment to bring justice and mercy to our sinful world by his death on the cross. But Jesus' death was not just a heroic act of self-sacrifice, of giving his life out of love for us. As his resurrection revealed, it is a passage to a new and everlasting life that he invites us to share even now through the gift of the Holy Spirit. This is a grace or power that enables us to live a life of love and to build a just and merciful society

Another important theme that courses through the Bible is what I would call the distorted perception of reality. The Bible virtually begins with it in the Garden Story. This seemingly simple story tackles a key challenge that all human beings face: to accept being a creature rather than try to become the creator. God instructs the couple that they may eat any tree but one. All relationships operate within appropriate boundaries or frameworks and within the story this instruction establishes the appropriate boundary. The temptation is to cross it on our terms (eat the fruit of the tree) in the belief that we will then be in control (you will be like God). This is the dream of the modern consumer: unlimited supply that will satisfy any demand. The irony is that the couple end up erecting all kinds of barriers between themselves (hiding their nakedness behind fig leaves) and God (hiding from God among the trees). Same God and same couple, but what was seen beforehand as good (God, themselves) is now seen as evil and to be feared. This distorted perception occurs in the Gospels where one group who see Jesus heal someone proclaim it as a work of God, whereas another group, seeing the same thing, claim it is a work of the devil. With such a distorted perception of reality, how can human beings establish true justice and mercy? But God is good and loyal and comes to restore our true perception of things, and so we have the story of Israel culminating in the figure of Jesus. In a definitive response to the serpent's bogus claim 'eat this and you will be like God' Jesus proclaims 'those who eat my flesh and drink my blood have eternal life'. In an echo of Gen 1:26, we will finally be remade in the image and likeness of our just and merciful God.

Hopefully, these few introductory remarks and the reflections that follow will be of some use to readers who celebrate the Lord's day, whether as preachers in the liturgy who need to prepare a homily, or worshippers in our churches who listen to the readings. They may also be of some use to any who are curious about what the Bible has to say to our world.

Introduction to the Gospel of Matthew (for Year A)

It may be useful for readers at this point to have a brief introduction to the Gospel according to Matthew. Each of the four gospels provides a somewhat different (and limited) angle on Jesus; human beings, even inspired ones, cannot say everything that could be said about Jesus (cf the remark in John 21:25).[1] Matthew, like Luke but unlike Mark and John, commences with an account of Jesus' birth, follows this with an account of his public ministry mainly in Galilee, and concludes with his death and resurrection. A significant feature of Matthew's understanding of Jesus is that he is the one who fulfils Old Testament prophecies and whose teaching completes the Torah or law (cf Jesus' remark on Torah/law and prophecy in 5:17, part of the 'sermon on the mount'). You will find that Matthew's Gospel provides frequent references to prophetic and law texts, and debates with Jewish authorities about their meaning. The claim of Matthew's Gospel is that Jesus does not come to abolish the Torah but to fulfil it. The mystery of God is always unfolding its meaning in our world, a claim that is also made by the Old Testament. Important Old Testament titles such as Son of Man, Messiah/Christ, Son of David and Son of God are applied to Jesus and thereby assume a deeper meaning. While each title reveals something about his identity he transcends them all.

Matthew, and the other Gospels as well, never separate the person of Jesus from his teaching. His whole life—words and actions—proclaim his identity and mission to replace the false kingdom of Satan with the 'kingdom of heaven'. The most visible sign of its presence is of course Jesus himself, and the foundational church community that gathers around

---

1. Even more so this brief introduction. For further reading, Brendan Byrne's book on Matthew in the bibliography is recommended.

him. Another important, and difficult, aspect of Matthew's account is that the revelation of God's purpose in the figure of Jesus triggers hostility and rejection, in particular among Jewish authorities. As this grows, Matthew's Gospel presents Jesus instructing his disciples about the nature of the kingdom (cf in particular the prominence of parables from chapter 13 on) and warning them of his impending death. Contemporary scholarship holds that the Gospel was written in the late first century CE and may well reflect not only Jesus' own experience but also the deepening rift between Judaism and early Christianity. Hostility is signalled early in Matthew's infancy narrative (Herod's massacre of the children) and reaches its climax in the plot to kill Jesus when he enters the holy city Jerusalem and preaches authoritatively in the temple. In a last supper with the disciples, he provides them with the gift of himself in the eucharistic bread and wine before suffering a violent and humiliating death. While those who regard themselves as insiders (chief priests, scribes, elders) mock the one who has been finally 'eliminated', those who are regarded as outsiders (the centurion and his squad) profess 'Truly this man was God's Son'. This serves as another signal in the Gospel for what is to come. In the final scene (28:16–20), the now resurrected Son of God entrusts his universal mission to the disciples—the embryonic church. The ones who had themselves rejected and abandoned him to a man are still the chosen and trusted ones; an assurance that reconciliation and healing are offered to all no matter how distant they may see themselves, or how others may see them, in relation to Jesus.

First Sunday of Advent

Isaiah 2:1–5; Romans 13:11–14; Matthew 24:37–44

As we begin a new liturgical year the church gives us a gospel that talks about the end, or at least the end of this earthly age. This may initially appear a little surprising but there is a reason for it: if we reflect on the end of things a bit we may be better prepared to launch into the new liturgical year and be more confident about the future. In other words it is likely there is more to this talk about our end than initially meets the eye and our readings should help us see something of it.

Jesus likening himself to a burglar provides a good starting point; if you offered people a selection of images of Jesus I doubt whether this one would be a favourite. Yet it makes two important points. The first is that there is no point trying to keep this burglar out of your 'house'; he is quite unlike any other burglar and can break in at any time, anywhere. So you might as well accept this and get a good night's sleep. Stop worrying. Why then the injunction to 'stay awake'? Again I think there is more here than initially meets the eye. The gospel passage begins with Jesus saying that the Son of Man is surely coming to bring God's purpose to an end or completion even though people may never give it a thought or reject it altogether. The great flood came because it was part of God's purpose irrespective of what people thought and, according to Jesus' version of it, most had no idea or couldn't give a toss. Furthermore, when Jesus comes it will be with a definite purpose, although to the unknowing or uncaring eye it will look like sheer chance, no apparent reason why 'of two men in the fields one is taken, one left'.

Within this context the injunction to 'stay awake' does not mean all night vigils. Rather, it means we should take care to keep two important things in mind. The first is that even though it may not look like it from a human perspective, God is bringing the divine purpose for creation to its completion in God's good time. This should fuel hope. The second thing is that God knows exactly how and where we fit in and play our role in advancing the divine purpose (life is not chance or chaos). This should fuel faith. It also allows a second point to be made about Jesus as burglar. Unlike the common or garden variety prowling our suburbs, Jesus breaks into our 'houses' only for our good, not to rob or take away but to give, not to kill but to bestow life, not to instil fear but to tell us not to be afraid and to assure us that we are all invited to share in the kingdom of his father, our true home. Jesus will even invade the houses of those who most fear him and want to keep him as far away as possible, hoping that his words may convince them to change their lives.

Second Sunday of Advent

Isaiah 11:1–10; Romans 15:4–9; Matthew 3:1–12

I wonder how we would react if a person got up in church and spoke—as a new message—those words from Isaiah in the first reading. Would we welcome it or require an implementation 'time-line' beforehand? And what if a figure like John the Baptist appeared—again for the first time—dressed in strange clothes and shouting at us about the urgent need to repent as he does in today's gospel reading. Would we listen or insist first on a decent dress code for speakers in church? Is it because we are so familiar with these passages that we have in a sense 'domesticated' them? Or is it because we think, or have been schooled to think, that the period of revelation was a 'special' almost magic time when these kinds of things happened? And, thank God, that period is over and we do not expect anything like that now. We live in the 'post–revelation' period where things are supposed to be stable and certainly not shocking.

But the same Spirit that stirred Isaiah and John is still in our midst and presumably still stirring the pot. And when you look at the core of their messages it is as fresh and as challenging today as it was in their day. What Isaiah sees that Israel (and the world) needs, and what he believes will happen in God's good time, is the establishment of God's justice. For the Judean monarchy in which he lived, this was embodied above all in the anointed king (Hebrew: *messiah*) who implemented God's justice and made right judgments, as the passage emphasises. If and when this happens, Isaiah believes that Jerusalem, the holy mountain, will become like a marvellous farmyard where the most unlikely crew—domestic animals, wild animals and the farmer's kids—all get on famously together. Not only that, all the nations will want to join in. In a word, it is all about relationships and in our global 'village' the ability to get on together becomes ever more crucial.

If Isaiah hopes for the perfect society, John the Baptist challenges his audience with one of the crucial necessities that will bring it about—change, or the appropriate gospel term, repentance (there is nothing necessarily positive about change in itself). This can be hard for those who are part of the establishment; in the gospel passages these are the Pharisees and Sadducees whom John singles out and challenges. The tendency is to think that it is the others who need change and repentance. Do we Christians tend to fall into this category at times, tending to think that we have got it together and it is the others who need to change? When I was growing up, the guilty outsiders were the communists, now it seems to be secular society. Whatever the case, John's call to change may be even more urgent now than in his own day and affects us all, both 'insiders' and 'outsiders'. Modern society faces major challenges on a number of fronts—abortion, medical ethics, family, environment, politics, etc.

If I am right then these texts that, from certain points of view, can appear alien and even 'ridiculous' are targeting two very basic things: the challenge to repent and to love one another. They look very ordinary but, as we know, they are in reality very radical because these are the hardest things to do, and to do consistently. It is hard to admit failure and our responsibility for it (repentance) and it is hard to ask forgiveness from those we have wronged (we need to trust them, love them and hope in them). But, as Paul says in the passage from Romans, 'Everything that was written long ago in the Scriptures was meant to teach us something about hope'. These texts are in the Bible because God knows that we can do it, providing we trust in the help that God provides. Otherwise there would be no point having them in the Bible. We are called to be fully Christian and to build a fully Christian society on this earth but not for our sakes only, as Paul takes care to point out. Ultimately, the greatest thing we can do in our individual and community lives is 'to give glory to God', to show forth the powerful presence of God in our midst.

Third Sunday of Advent

Isaiah 35:1–6, 10; James 5:7–10; Matthew 11:2–11

Prophets and prophecy are the focus in this Sunday's readings: they begin with a prophecy from the book of Isaiah, the letter of James holds prophets up as an example of patience, and in the reading from Matthew Jesus responds to the troubled enquiry from John the Baptist. Prophets were in a vulnerable situation in society, particularly when they proclaimed future judgment or salvation. They had nothing to rely on except their conviction that they had been called to proclaim a message. Those who proclaimed God's judgment on a sinful people shortly before the exile could appeal to it as validation, or at least their disciples could. But, it is much trickier when it comes to predictions of salvation and a glorious future, as in today's first reading. Old Testament Prophets made these grand promises but most never lived to see them realised. Yet they stood by their words. What motivated them to do so? Above all, it must have been their faith in God and in their prophetic vocation. That God had called them to proclaim this word was confirmation enough that this word of God would be realised in God's good time. If not, they were following a sham god.

The Hebrew term for 'word' (*dabar*) can also mean thing and event. Hence the proclamation of a '*dabar*' of God is a word that, in the act of being proclaimed, is creating or bringing about the event of which it speaks. The prophet's task is to maintain fidelity to the one who commands that this creative word be spoken to the people. This is presumably what the letter of James refers to when it says 'For your example, brothers, in submitting with patience, take the prophets who spoke in the name of the Lord'. Prophets prophesied and then waited in patience like a farmer—yet they often never had the satisfaction of seeing the fruit. But prophecy, and discipleship in general, is about the fulfilment of God's word and God's purpose, not personal satisfaction.

But if one can say this about the prophets and hold them up as an example of faith and endurance, then we should also say the same about the people of Israel and hold them up as an example. Because it was they who preserved the prophet's words long after his or her death and bequeathed them to us in the books that we now read. In that sense, they were just as inspired as the prophets.

For all their admirable patience and faith, prophets had their doubts at times. Jeremiah wonders about his vocation and Elisha is unsure whether or not he has received the spirit of Elijah in 2 Kings 2. Even worse, he initially botches the job of raising the son of the great lady of Shunem in 2 Kings 4. The reading from Matthew's Gospel records the doubts of the greatest of the prophets, John the Baptist. He believed he had been commissioned to announce the kingdom of heaven as a great judgment and here is his promised judge handing out favours to all and sundry. The striking thing about Jesus' comments on John is that he holds up the doubting, questioning baptiser as a model prophet, indeed more than a prophet. John's doubts and questions arise precisely because he is so loyal to his vocation and his convictions about the message he preaches, and it is this to which Jesus draws the attention of his listeners. What is more, true loyalty to one's vocation from God is not a rigid loyalty; it is open to whatever God wants one to say or do, not what one would prefer God to say or do. So Jesus can send John's disciples back with a message that challenges John to revise his expectations, confident that John will accept it. John and his doubts and questions can help us accept that we receive more than we ever make, we are gifted with more than we can ever give, we are found rather than we find, discovered rather than we discover. We tend to try and make God in our image but Jesus comes to make us in God's image.

Jesus' final comment raises another important point about prophetic preaching and discipleship in general. One's vocation is not about personal status or satisfaction but about advancing the kingdom of heaven, and one's perfection lies in being loyal to this above all else. Prophecy, priesthood, parenthood, etc are there for the sake of populating the kingdom of heaven; hence the least in the kingdom is greater than any prophet, priest or king—and prophets, priests and kings who enter the kingdom will no doubt be the first to affirm this.

Fourth Sunday of Advent

Isaiah 7:10–14; Romans 1:1–7; Matthew 1:18–25

One of the more comforting aspects of our faith is that the gospels link Jesus via Joseph to the dodgy Davidic dynasty. You only have to open the books of Kings and read some stories about the Davidic monarchy to realise how many of its members are censured or condemned and how few are praised. In our reading from Isaiah we are given a glimpse of king Ahaz who, according to 2 Kings 16:2—4 was a bad lad indeed. As the verses preceding our Isaiah reading tell it, Ahaz is under siege from a northern coalition of Israel (the northern kingdom) and Syria (Aram) and he is scared ('the heart of Ahaz . . . shook like the trees of the forest before the wind'). In place of fear, Isaiah urges trust in God ('if you do not stand firm in faith, you will not stand at all'). I wonder whether there is a hint of sarcasm in Isaiah's offer to ask for a sign 'as deep as sheol or as high as heaven'.

We know from the Kings text that Ahaz sought protection from the Assyrian superpower in the crisis: something of this may lie behind his evasive reply. Isaiah knows his man and the fears and self-interest that drives him. His announcement of God's decision shows that God was already planning protection for Judah against the invaders: 'the young woman *is* with child and shall bear a son, and shall name him Immanuel (God-with-us)'. God is with the chosen people to bring about what is best for them but this may not be what Ahaz or the people have in mind at the time. The comforting thing about trawling through the Davidic dynasty is that Jesus was apparently quite happy to own them all as his ancestors; the bad as well as the good. The implication of this is that he is also happy to own us, despite all the bad we do. Surely a powerful motive to put away our fears.

According to our reading from Matthew's Gospel, Joseph too was faced with a crisis that made him afraid and prompted him to make a decision.

But Joseph redeems the Davidic line here. Unlike Ahaz, his fears were for Mary his betrothed, not for himself and his reputation. The angelic messenger plays the same role as Isaiah to Ahaz and urges him not to be afraid and to change his mind, to see God's presence in a situation that Joseph's culture would view as a disgrace. The basis for making this change adds an important element to the theology of Immanuel (God–with–us): the sign that God is indeed with us is that the child will be called Jesus (saviour) and that salvation will involve freeing his people from their sins. For readers of the gospel, 'his people' are all those who accept Jesus; through him God is with us all, both Jew and Gentile. The way Paul puts it in the reading from Romans, all the nations are called 'to belong to Jesus Christ', that is, to become one family of God's beloved children.

All of us I think welcome the notion that God is with us but what are our thoughts about this seemingly simple and comforting statement as we approach the feast of Christmas? The thrust of the Bible, both Old and New Testaments, is that God is with us, completely and unconditionally. Despite all the failings of Israel in the Old Testament and the disciples in the New Testament, God never gives up on them. But there is of course another side to this statement that we need to take on board if we are serious about it. Given that God is completely with and for us, we need to be completely with and for God. We do not need to be like this for God to love us; we can only love God because God first loved us. But our response to that divine love should be to give our all to God. Our attempts to be loving may look pretty inadequate to us at times but Paul testifies in his letter to the Romans that the grace of Christ turned him from a hater of the church into a devoted lover and preacher of the good news. When we fear that our love is inadequate, we need to remember that the grace of Christ makes it—our love—delightful and precious in God's eyes.

Christmas

Midnight Mass: Isaiah 9:1–7; Titus 2:1–14; Luke 2:1–14

It is appropriate that Luke's account of the birth of Jesus gets pride of place in the readings for Christmas—at both the midnight and dawn masses. It is the most detailed account and is fascinating for the contrast it draws between our world and God's. Luke begins with the census decreed by Caesar Augustus and how the chain of command in the vast Roman bureaucracy operates to implement the emperor's word. It works its way out from the centre through 'officials' to the boundaries of the empire. One has the impression that Luke understands the Roman world pretty well and is not hostile to it. In many ways it is a familiar world to us moderns and our own vast bureaucracies. The number of people who commute each day to work in an office; the intricate chains of command; the names and numbers on computer screens that hopefully correspond to real people out there with their needs and demands. When the boss cracks the whip to get something done, we jump to it. So it is in Luke's world; the chain of command reaches out from Rome to touch an unknown couple in a distant small corner of the empire and they set out to comply with the census decree. And, like our own systems that sometimes break down, Joseph and Mary 'fall through the cracks' of the Roman system and end up without accommodation. And Mary is expecting her first child.

Luke may respect Roman institutions but he sees their limitations. It is at this point that he develops his powerful contrast between the two worlds. Where the Roman world is focused on the centre—the emperor—God is focused on what that world would regard as irrelevant, the fringes. The seemingly insignificant couple Mary and Joseph and their baby become the moment and the locus of a decisive divine action. Whereas the chain of command in the Roman world operates only through tried and tested officials, God's chain of command trusts everyone. God's angel does not go scouring the earth to find a trustworthy messenger of the good news of Jesus' birth: the nearest ones, a bunch of shepherds, will do just fine. Whereas Roman bureaucracy—and ours as well?—maintains loyalty through fear of penalties, the angel's first word to the shepherds is 'do not fear'. Whereas bureaucracies carefully guard their business deals from prying eyes, God has no secrets. The good news of the birth of the saviour is 'to be shared by the whole people'. Whereas the nations of the world measure their worth in terms of power and wealth, the worth of God's world is measured by a helpless baby. Finally, and it's a nice Lucan touch, the shepherds (and the reader) are given a glimpse of the heavenly 'office' (the real 'holy office') where it's party time; the whole heavenly host singing and praising God and rejoicing in the good fortune of us lowly human beings.

As well as drawing a contrast between the busyness of Caesar's host and the heavenly host, there may be another point to Luke's account here. The Roman empire had to set in train a complex and lengthy process to find out how many people there were under the emperor's rule; how many over whom he had to maintain control. In contrast, God does not need a census, knowing each creature immediately and intimately; and not for the purpose of exercising control over them but in order to free them from the kind of slavery that human beings impose on others. The shepherds are free to decide whether they will go to Bethlehem or not: they make their decision 'Let us go to Bethlehem and see this thing'. So it is with everyone that the saviour Jesus encounters both in his earthly and resurrected life: he frees us from the things that enslave us, that breed fear and hostility, so that we can make responsible decisions and that is surely what being human means. If we make free responsible decisions like the shepherds and act on them then, like the shepherds, we become part of the treasured staff of that heavenly 'office'; note how Luke's account of the shepherds' glorifying and praising God 'for all that they had heard and seen' echoes closely his earlier description of the heavenly host.

Christmas

Vigil Mass: Isaiah 62:1–5; Acts 13:16–17, 22–25;
Matthew 1:1–25 or Matthew 1:18–25
Dawn Mass: Isaiah 62:11–12; Titus 3:4–7 Luke 2:15–20
Mass During the Day: Isaiah 52:7–10; Hebrews 1:1–6; John 1:1–18

One of the most striking features of the readings for Christmas is how differently the gospels describe the 'advent' of Jesus. Matthew prefaces his account with a genealogy that reaches back to Israel's father in faith, Abraham and culminates in Joseph, descendant of the house of David and betrothed to Mary. Luke sets his account of the birth of Jesus in the context of a census of 'the whole world' decreed by the Roman emperor. The prologue to John's Gospel portrays Jesus as the coming into the world of the heavenly, creative word of God. Each of the gospel accounts unveils a key aspect of the meaning of Christmas for us.

Matthew's account, as I read it, announces Jesus as the one who heals time—our broken individual lives, the frayed threads of the history of Israel and the house of David, the fragmented histories of peoples of all times and places. Matthew's genealogy is just too neat to be true, and no one knows this better than Matthew. On the surface he provides us with a perfectly structured three-fold set of fourteen generations but let's look beneath the surface a little. In the first set of fourteen generations, the names that catch the eye are those of women and, when one reads the stories about them, they are unusual women to say the least. There is Tamar who begot children by her father-in-law Judah (Gen 38), Rahab the prostitute (Josh 2), and Ruth the Moabite (according to Deuteronomy 23 Moabites and Ammonites were to be forbidden entry to Israel's liturgy; they epitomised the unworthy 'foreigner'). In the second set we have Bathsheba; David raped her and had her husband Uriah, the foreigner, murdered. Then there is Solomon whose infidelities, according to 1 Kings 11, caused the fragmentation of David's kingdom; readers can consult the accounts of subsequent divisive and disobedient scions of David such as Rehoboam, Abijam, Ahaz (the target of Isaiah's censure), and Manasseh (a very bad egg indeed, according to 2 Kings 21). We know little about most of the figures in the third set of fourteen generations because, in comparison to their pre-exilic ancestors, they were apparently nobodies on the stage of history. None of them were able to restore royal rule: they are like the frayed ends of the Davidic line. Yet, these figures are all an integral part of Jesus' Jewish ancestry and Jesus gladly owns them all, just as he embraces and heals the fragmented lives of our present generation and reaches out to all generations to come. As the angel says, 'he will save his people from their sins': *his* people are all God's people. For Matthew, Jesus is the only one who can forge a perfect genealogy or family of humanity out of its feuding factions.

In Luke's account the emphasis is on place. We live our earthly lives in time and place; just as time can unite or divide humanity so can place. Place plays such an important symbolic role in our relationships with one another: as the real estate agents say 'it's about location, location, and location'. One can hardly imagine a greater 'distance' than that between the Emperor Augustus in Rome, the centre of the then known world, and Mary and Joseph in far away Bethlehem—and not even in Bethlehem itself but apparently in a shepherd's refuge or hut outside the town. This is living beyond the fringes. Yet the baby born in this 'no-place' is the one who, in Luke's story, replaces the emperor as the central person at the centre of the world. But, in doing so Jesus effectively abolishes any sense of privilege or superiority that people attribute to themselves or others because they happen to occupy a certain position at a certain time. Anyone, anywhere and at anytime is able to become a treasured and loved disciple. Time and place retain their importance because they are the arena of the incarnation, our human arena. But the incarnation takes place or is meant to take place in the heart of every human being who lives his/her time and in his/her place.

If Matthew and Luke break down the barriers of time and place or rewrite their meaning, we might say that John's prologue abolishes a third barrier that human beings erect, and it is the most important one—the divide between heaven and earth. We tend to think that God inhabits another 'world', the heavenly realm that is totally alien to ours. Every now and then God condescends to appear in our world. But I think John sets out to correct this perception. It arises because of the 'sin of the world', an affliction that causes a distorted perception of ourselves and of God. But John teaches, 'all that came to be had life in him'. This Word of God, the Word that is God in whom we have life 'was coming (always) into the world' which is 'his own domain' and he 'lived among us' as one of us. There are not two separate worlds or, if in our distorted perception there are, God's purpose is to show us that there is really only one, God's 'world' in which we are to 'become children of God'. For John, Jesus is the only one who can remove the barriers that impede our vision; then we will be able to see the glory of God in Jesus, the Word of God who is with us and has always been with us as he has always been with God. To put this another way, God became in our image and likeness in order to show us that we are in the image and likeness of God.

Holy Family (Sunday after Christmas)

Sirach 3:2–6, 12–14; Colossians 3:12–21; Matthew 2:13–15, 19–23

This reading from Matthew's Gospel concludes what we may call the story of the 'Holy Family'. There is a brief reference to Jesus' mother and brothers at the end of chapter 12 but, significantly, their request to see Jesus prompts him to describe the new family of discipleship that he has been sent to form. When we look a little more closely at Matthew's cryptic account of Jesus' birth and childhood what stands out is the series of fulfilments of Old Testament prophecies. As scholars have pointed out these combine with the opening genealogy to portray Jesus not only as a son of Abraham (the genealogy), but as Immanuel (God–with–us) in 1:23, Son of David in 2:6, the new Moses in 2:15, a new Jeremiah in 2:18 (cf Jer 31:15), and probably a new Samson in 2:23. This last reference is somewhat unsure because there is no Old Testament text that corresponds to the quote in 2:23 except perhaps the reference to Samson in Judges 13:5, 7. If this is the case, then Matthew has imaginatively linked the Hebrew term *nazir* (consecrated) to the town of Nazareth.

It is clear that Matthew has shaped his introduction to his Gospel to evoke key figures in the Old Testament and to allude to some key texts associated with them. Thus the account of the flight into Egypt and Herod's massacre of children around Bethlehem (omitted from our reading) is designed to evoke Moses and the exodus. The reason for this presumably is that Matthew's subsequent account will show how Jesus incorporates and at the same time transcends the significance of these great Old Testament figures. This in turn provides a clue about the purpose of his portrayal of the 'Holy Family'. The focus is clearly on Jesus and not on Mary and Joseph: their roles are to advance God's purpose as revealed in the child Jesus. Within Matthew's Gospel one could say that this purpose is expressed most clearly in the passage referred to above: Matthew 12:46–50. God's purpose, and that of Jesus, is to establish a new family of disciples; the brothers and sisters of Jesus. It is a striking feature of Jesus' ministry and the early church that no privileged role is given to members of Jesus' extended family: they seem to have been absorbed into the new family of the church. So different to the prominent position given to members of Moses' family (Miriam the prophet, Aaron the priest) in the Torah and to the family of Mohammed in Islam.

Does this mean that the importance of the 'Holy Family' and the family in general is demeaned in Christianity and does this create problems for the church's mission in our world? It seems to me that Christians must find their primary family among the disciples of Jesus ('unless you hate father or mother you cannot be my disciple', and 'where two or three are gathered together in my name there I am in the midst of them'). On the one hand this means that it does not matter whether you come from a stable family with a mum and dad or not. All disciples are equally members of the family of Jesus, no matter what their background may be. On the other hand, one can also say that the natural family of mum, dad and the kids can only find its true identity and purpose within the context of the family of disciples. One might like to see the passage from Colossians as a portrait of how this family should live. If one treats discipleship as a handy accessory that can be 'added on' to my family and career, then the gospel warns that such discipleship will wither and die. In seeking to do so, the members of the family are like Mary and Joseph who learned that they had to place their commitment to Jesus and his mission above any expectations that they may have had of their marriage and family plans.

If this is a fair interpretation of the gospel message then it singles out marriage and the family as the truly heroic vocation of our age—at least. Parents (and their children) are called to act on the conviction that their true identity as a family is to be found, not within their own circle and its interests, but within that of discipleship of Jesus—and the disciples of Jesus are not to be identified exclusively with the members of the church. They are called to do this in a world that tends to speak of career rather than vocation, of status rather than service, of the 'nuclear family' rather than the family of humanity, and that sees religion as a private matter, a useful 'add-on' for weekends perhaps. Families that seek to live the vocation of the 'Holy Family' are foregoing a powerful and seductive view of family life for the sake of the gospel.

Mary Mother of God

Numbers 6:22–27; Galatians 4:4–7; Luke 2:16–21

The famous blessing in Numbers that Aaron and his sons are to pronounce over the people of Israel celebrates the greatest boundary 'violation' that the Old Testament could conceive: God dwelling on earth among the people. It is a big moment and the Old Testament provides a long prelude to it.

The Bible begins with a story of boundary violation; Adam and Eve wanting to transcend the human condition and be like God. Paradoxically, this boundary violation creates a barrier between them and God from whom they now hide. Just before the flood story, there is in Genesis 6:1–4 a brief report about the 'sons of God' begetting children via the 'daughters of men'. The report is cryptic but the message is clear enough: this mixing of the divine and human is just not on for the Old Testament, partly because rituals of this kind went on in the cultures round about Israel. The Torah spends considerable effort to ensure that the people know their place in relation to God and keep it. Yet in a typical Torah move, once appropriate boundaries have been established between God and Israel so that Israel knows its place as God's creature, though chosen by God, the text sets about showing how certain ones can be crossed on God's authority: intimacy with God on God's terms. Moses, Aaron and 70 representatives of the people are invited to ascend mount Sinai and dine in God's presence. Then, in a climactic move (Exod 25:8), Moses is instructed to build a sanctuary so that God may dwell in Israel's midst—God pitches his tent (*shekinah*) among the Israelites in order to bring them blessing.

Despite the intimacy symbolised by the tabernacle/tent (God's dwelling) in the midst of Israel, the feast that we celebrate today would be regarded in Old Testament eyes as the ultimate boundary violation between divine and human, a kind of revisiting of Genesis 6:1–4. The notion that a woman could be the mother of God is an extraordinary, even outrageous, one when you think about it. How can the time-bound, location-bound and fleeting human life of a woman mother an infinite, eternal, transcendent God? Yet it is due in part to the Old Testament conviction that the transcendent God is thereby able to be completely immanent (and vice-versa) that Christianity is in turn able to articulate its belief that Mary as the mother of Jesus is thereby also the mother of God.

The Church's proclamation about Mary also stems from its faith proclamation about Jesus. Because we believe he is God, Mary as his mother must therefore be the mother of God (in the Greek church the preferred term is *theotokos* or 'God-bearer'). Our belief that Mary is the virgin mother of Jesus acknowledges the divine initiative in his conception and his divinity. Hence the frequent use of the phrase 'the virgin mother of God'.

In an important way therefore, the feast of Mary as the mother of God celebrates the removal of the last boundary or barrier between the divine and the human—done of course on God's initiative, not ours. Its removal does not mean that the difference between human and divine is blurred or obliterated. Far from it. According to the Old Testament narratives, the attempt to transcend the human condition on our terms ends up creating more problems than it solves. We become more divided from God and from ourselves. Ironically, in our desire to transcend boundaries or barriers between ourselves and the person or thing we desire we end up erecting more in their place. When God removes these barriers through the life and grace of Christ, we are finally able to see ourselves and our relationship with God in its true light, not the distorted feeble light of our own making.

Another important aspect of Mary as mother of God is that she exemplifies the dynamic purpose of this relationship between God and ourselves. Being the mother of God involved her full cooperation in the purpose of God; in other words, her discipleship ('let it be done to me according to your word'). Luke notes on several occasions that Mary 'treasured all these things and pondered on them in her heart'. As mother, Mary conceived the Word of God in her womb and brought him forth for the world. Jesus, as son of God and son of Mary gives his life in order to make us sons and daughters of God. Hence, she is not only the mother of God but our mother as well. As disciple, Mary conceives the word of God in her heart and brings it forth in her life for the world. She is not only the faithful disciple of Jesus but our model of discipleship as well.

The Epiphany

Isaiah 60:1–6; Ephesians 3:2–3, 5–6; Matthew 2:1–12

Most of us have had the experience of cruising along on our chosen path of life when, somewhat unexpectedly, a person appears whose presence we sense may have massive implications for our life. Do we welcome this person as someone from whom we can learn and hopefully change, or do we see him or her as a rival whose potential influence needs to be countered or eliminated in some way? The more we see ourselves as like a 'king' or 'queen' in our domain, the more we may feel we have to gain from the newcomer—or lose.

The contrast between Matthew's portrayal of the three wise men and king Herod fits rather well into this scenario. The 'epiphany', the manifestation or appearance of Jesus, poses a challenge to those with power and prestige. The wise men are evidently men of standing and wealth in their society and Matthew does not give their number. The traditional number of three is presumably derived from the three gifts (gold, frankincense and myrrh) that they offer the Christ child. But Matthew may have envisaged a considerable number, a large group of prestigious foreigners that would cause a stir in Herod's kingdom. They come to pay the newborn child homage, are overwhelmed with joy on seeing him and immediately fulfill their commitment. This is the one who will bring true wisdom to the world and they are ready to acknowledge their dependence on him and his teaching.

In contrast, the reaction of Herod to the wise men and their news is one of fear, because they refer to the newborn child as 'the infant king of the Jews'. I come from a farming background and there is a saying among farmers that there is never enough room for two bulls in the same paddock. Herod is king of the Jews and he is not about to share his domain with another, much less hand it over. Hence, he must move immediately, in a deceptive way, to eliminate what he sees as a rival. But of course, as Matthew portrays Jesus, he is no threat to Herod's earthly kingdom; Jesus is the one who comes to enable all, in whatever path of life they walk, whether it be as a servant or a ruler, to achieve their full humanity as sons and daughters of God.

But, in order to fulfill this mission, Jesus must manifest himself to all, even those who reject him and kill him. The fact that his epiphany or appearance is not a threat to anyone but rather their salvation is graphically demonstrated in the way he prays for and forgives those who put him to death. The epiphany of Jesus caused Herod to be afraid and to plan to eliminate the 'other' king whom he saw as the source of his fear. But Jesus comes to take away our fear and enable divided humanity to build a new community based on love and trust. As the letter to the Ephesians puts it so well 'it means that pagans now share the same inheritance, that they are parts of the same body, in Christ Jesus'.

In principle, we are all ready and willing to accept the 'manifestation' of Jesus in our lives because we believe, in the words of Isaiah, that he is the light that has come, the glory of the Lord rising in our midst. But of course, it can be tricky to discern just where this presence of Jesus is being made manifest in our lives and in what form. We might think that, after 2,000 years of tradition, we know the score pretty well. But, the Word of God is 'ever old and ever new' and has an uncanny knack of surprising us and catching us out. We pray for the wisdom of the wise men to discern the presence of our king and to welcome him into our lives; his presence may not take the form we want but it may be the one we need.

Baptism of the Lord

Isaiah 42:1–4, 6–7a; Acts 10:34–38; Matthew 3:13–17

Two key elements of the Bible's portrayal of God are transcendence and immanence. Only an utterly transcendent God can also be completely immanent, reaching anyone at any time anywhere. By the same token, a God who is completely immanent, totally present to me at this moment, must also be completely transcendent, otherwise a fake god. The feast of the Baptism of Jesus celebrates the immanent side with a vengeance, so much so that Matthew's account (as do the other evangelists' accounts in different ways) hastens at strategic points to signal Jesus' transcendence. It would seem that the tradition about Jesus' baptism both enthralled and disturbed the early church. How could the son of God participate fully in a rite that identified you as a repentant sinner, at a distance, as it were, from God?

The first signal comes with Matthew's report that John the Baptist tried to dissuade Jesus by proclaiming that he was the one in need of baptism, not Jesus. Jesus' reply combines two things. One is that John's rite of baptism is in no way to be changed for him—he will be baptised like everybody else. The second signals what his baptism means, it is in order to 'do all that righteousness demands'. It is a sign of Jesus' complete commitment to God's will to bring about righteousness for humanity. Hence, Jesus joins in solidarity with all sinners to provide the freedom from sin that the washing in water signifies. As the preface for the feast expresses it: 'Jesus was baptised in waters made holy by the one who was baptised'.

The second signal accompanies Jesus' emergence from the Jordan: the heavens are opened and Jesus sees the Spirit descending like a dove. Although in the scene that Matthew constructs Jesus is the only one to see the dove, the reader is made privy to this 'private revelation', thereby being assured that Jesus' entry into the 'tomb' of the water is the work of the transcendent God in heaven. The third signal is the voice of God that follows. The addressee is unspecified and so open–ended but the purpose of the voice is to identify the one who has expressed complete solidarity with sinners as 'my Son, the Beloved'.

In a subtle touch, these words of God allude to the famous text on the 'servant' in the book of Isaiah, our first reading (the Greek word *pais* can double as 'servant' and 'son'). It is a most appropriate allusion because of the way the manner and goal of the servant's mission are outlined. Given that, in its Old Testament context, this text refers to Israel, the description of its mission marks a massive shift away from the traditional notion of how God (and Israel) deals with foreign nations. Customary expectations of conquest and glory are overturned. Likewise, the manner of Jesus' mission shocked his contemporaries, prompting John the Baptist to send a delegation to ask whether Jesus was indeed the one whose coming he proclaimed, and prompting Peter to remonstrate with Jesus ('Lord, this must never happen to you').

In a similar vein, the goal of the servant Israel's mission is not to mount a throne of power and prestige but to enter the dark dungeons of the nations, to free captives and let people see the light. The goal of Jesus' mission, whom we believe fulfills the mission of Isaiah's servant, is nicely captured by Peter's words in the second reading from Acts. God 'does not have favourites' and loves all equally. Peter has come to this conviction via his own, at times, troubling experience as a disciple and by witnessing how 'Jesus went about doing good and curing all who had fallen into the power of the devil'.

The highly condensed references to Father, Son and Spirit in Matthew's account of the baptism point to another important theological element. In the rite of baptism, our immersion in water and emergence from it signifies the discarding of our 'old' sinful life and the putting on of a 'new' life that is a sharing in the life of the Trinity. Father Son and Holy Spirit are equally involved (immanent) in freeing us from our sinful selves in order that we may become heirs to the their divine (transcendent) life.

First Sunday of Lent

Genesis 2:7–9; 3:1–7; Romans 5:12–19 or 5:12, 17–19;
Matthews 4:1–11

That first reading from Genesis is about us, that we are all suckers for the advertising blurb in one way or another, all enslaved in some way to the seduction of sin. The season of Lent reminds us of this, painfully at times, but also offers the promise of liberation from our enslavement. In reading the 'Garden Story' I follow the modern view that it is about humanity as such; it reflects the mythical way of philosophising via storytelling before the advent of the philosophical treatise. The story form offers more flexibility in some ways than formal argument; as well as this it is always helpful to illustrate an argument with examples (stories). Our Old Testament story supplies both the example and the argument. The serpent's spiel represents that clever sales pitch that we fall for even as we protest we have seen through it (buy this and you will look divine; eat this and you will live to a 100; read this and I swear you will never see things the same way again). The ironical outcome of the couple's acceptance of this sales pitch is that things indeed are no longer seen the same way. Humanity's attempt to transcend its condition or situation on its own terms (to be free) leads to its opposite. The couple that hoped to be 'like God' behaves in a very ungodlike way, as frightened, vulnerable creatures who hide from each other behind leaves. Likewise, they try to hide from God, but in vain because God comes looking for them.

The message of the story is that one cannot escape this troubled situation by one's own efforts; to try and do so is simply to re-enact the story in one's own life. Our human condition is an enslavement from which we need to be delivered. The one who can deliver us must be supremely free in the biblical sense, where freedom means that one has a right relationship with God and that this relationship infuses all other relationships. Matthew's account of Jesus' temptation in the desert portrays him as the righteous one who, though tempted in every way that we are, remains supremely free because he maintains a right relationship with God.

In typical storytelling fashion, there are three temptations (three examples) that provide a torah or instruction for readers. The first clearly echoes the Garden Story with its temptation to transcend the human condition on one's own terms, to 'turn these stones into loaves'. Jesus' response to each temptation is to quote a passage from the torah (Deuteronomy) and to act in accord with it. In relation to the first temptation his response is to act only in accordance with God's will. The text's claim is that the words God has spoken in the Bible provide enough for us to decide what God's will is in our lives. We decide what God's will is because that is what God wants us to do: to listen to the Word and make an honest response. It is part of our dignity as God's children.

The second temptation attempts to get 'under' Jesus' reliance on God's word by targeting the trust on which it is based. The temptation to have experiential 'proof' that God cares and looks after us can be acute at times but its outcome, like the outcome of the failure of trust in the Garden story, is destructive. If a spouse continually seeks proof of the other's love, the relationship is likely to collapse under the pressure. How can you demand proof of love unless you first define what you mean by it, in which case you have taken control of the other person and demeaned and enslaved him or her? Jesus will not put God to the proof. The final temptation raises the question of an alternative to one's relationship with God. Can anything in this world justify such a move? The biblical answer is a resounding no! because of its conviction that no other relationships are really possible without a relationship to God. It forms the basis of all others and is the base on which God wants to build a rich human life.

As in the 'Garden Story', God comes looking for us as we hide in the garden, trying to escape—such is our distorted perception of God and ourselves. God not only wants to free us from our affliction and enslavement but to enrich us in a way that makes all the wealth of the world pale into insignificance. The reading from Romans underscores the difference via a series of statements 'if it is certain that . . . it is even more certain that . . . ' Seduced by the serpent, Eve and Adam saw God as mean, withholding what was their 'right'. In contrast Paul, who has been freed from his own enslavement by the grace of Christ, writes of the abundant gifts that God desires to shower on us. We need to face our sinfulness honestly and Lent is the season for this, but we also need—perhaps even more—to see it is a season in which our generous God seeks us out, bearing abundant gifts even though we do not deserve them.

Second Sunday of Lent

Genesis 12:1–4; 2 Timothy 1:8–10; Matthew 17:1–9

The transfiguration is a dramatic scene and its context in Matthew's Gospel is suitably dramatic; a telling one for the season of Lent (Mark's context is similar, Luke's somewhat different). It is preceded by Peter's confession of faith and Jesus' subsequent rebuke 'Get behind me, Satan' when Peter tries to dissuade Jesus from his purpose. Jesus then instructs the disciples about the nature of discipleship—it involves taking up one's cross and losing one's life. There is a sense of urgency and finality about the decision to follow Jesus because, as he goes on to say, the 'Son of Man' is to come and repay each one for his/her deeds; in fact this will happen to some of those present. Equally dramatically, the transfiguration is followed by the disciples' question about Elijah and Jesus' reply that Elijah has already come, has been rejected and persecuted, just as Jesus himself will be.

It is with good reason that Matthew sets the transfiguration as a beacon of blazing light in the midst of this apparent darkness. The very disciple whom a few verses before is referred to as 'Satan' gets to join his fishing partners on the mountain and see Jesus in glory, his shining face recalling the way Moses' face shone whenever he went into the tent of meeting (Ex 34). In the sermon on the mount, Jesus is the new Moses who proclaims a teaching that fulfils the purpose of the Torah. In the transfiguration on the mount, Jesus is again cast as the new Moses whose transformed visage and clothing signals the presence of God. And again there is continuity and fulfillment. Whereas Moses' face signaled the presence of God in the tent, the completely transfigured Jesus signals the presence of God—in him.

Understandably, Peter seeks to 'fit' Jesus within the established parameters of Torah and Prophecy and proposes three tents: one for Moses (Torah), one for Elijah (Prophets) and one for Jesus. But a tent is a temporary home for those on a journey whereas the journey and its goal has been reached on this mountain in the person of Jesus. He is the presence of God among us as indicated by the cloud (the sign of God's presence in the tent at Sinai and during the desert journey) and by the heavenly voice that identifies Jesus as 'my Son, the beloved'. The withdrawal of Moses and Elijah from the scene is another way of pointing to Jesus as the unique presence of God, as the one who now speaks the word of God. As once the people of Israel were enjoined to listen to the Torah (represented by Moses), and to Prophecy as its authentic proclamation and interpretation (represented by Elijah), so now they are to 'listen to him'.

The context of our gospel invites a further reflection. Is the 'world' portrayed on the mountain a kind of magical, ideal world whereas the real world, our world, is awaiting Jesus and the disciples when they descend the mountain? I don't think this is what Matthew has in mind. As he portrays it, the real world is the one with God on the mountain and Jesus descends the mountain to continue his work of transforming the 'unreal world' of sin and corruption that we have made. In God's eyes it is not fit for human habitation and God is bent on doing something about it.

As Lent comes round again we are challenged, however reluctantly, to face our flawed selves. It can be depressing to realise how little we have advanced since last year and that perhaps we have even regressed. The call to discipleship is indeed demanding and we fail—like Peter and like the disciples. Yet, like Satan Peter, we are invited up the mountain into the company of Jesus as the dwelling place of God. We may be afraid because of our inadequacies and our failures, we may fear that we will never be welcome in God's presence. But the gospel passage tells how Jesus comes and touches the disciples, assuring them 'not to be afraid'. The yearly return of the season of Lent assures us in its turn that this invitation is made again and again. It is never withheld because, as the second letter to Timothy says, 'this grace had already been granted to us in Christ Jesus, before the beginning of time'. The author of this letter, if it was Paul, is supremely confident that the power of God can transfigure us and enable us to step out of the shadows cast by our present and past and live by the light of Christ.

The transforming light of Christ that shines so warmly into the cold and dark of human lives is reflected nicely in the reading from Genesis 12, the text that tells how it all began. The call of Abraham is also set within a context of darkness and human failure—the stories of Genesis 2—11. Abraham's mission is to be the bearer of blessing to all the families of the earth. The story of Israel begins on a positive note; the mission will succeed. The only negative note is struck by the remark that—in the Hebrew—'I will bless those who bless you, the *one* who curses you I will curse'. This text envisages the overwhelming majority enjoying God's blessing.

Third Sunday of Lent

Exodus 17:3–7; Romans 5:1–2, 5–8;
John 4:5–42 or 4:5–15, 19–26, 39, 40–42

One of the challenges of life is maintaining the right distinction between what I would call boundaries and barriers. As we know to our regret in the church, we need to respect appropriate boundaries so that mature and enduring relationships between men and women, laity and clergy, adults and children may flourish. But there are barriers that impede the formation of relationships and which should be removed. Our readings this Sunday deal with two key ones. The reading from Exodus tackles the barrier that is 'erected' when trust 'breaks down'. The reading from John's Gospel tackles the barrier of religion.

In our Exodus narrative, the people lose trust in the promise that God and Moses are leading them to freedom in the land—despite in the story having experienced deliverance at the sea. Trust can become vulnerable when challenged by fear (no water) or the unknown (the wilderness). Once trust starts to break down, the focus of attention shifts to oneself (note the reference to 'I' first, then the kids and the cattle). One also starts to blame the other in the relationship and to make demands: is the Lord with us or not? A distorted perception of Moses and God develops and this exacerbates the sense of a barrier or distance between the people and God. One story even has the people prefer slavery in Egypt over journeying with God through the desert, such is their distorted perception of reality (Nb 11:4—6). The outcome of such a breakdown of trust is that one looks for another relationship: hence the golden calf apostasy at Sinai. The 'murmuring stories' paint a brutally honest portrait of ancient Israel, no doubt an urgent 'torah' for the reader about the importance of maintaining trust in God, even in the most desperate of circumstances (such as the exile).

If the Exodus text is about the erection of barriers that divide, the Gospel text from John is about the dismantling of them. The barrier between Jew and Samaritan ran deep; it affected even the most basic things that human beings need to share, such as water. In response to Jesus' initiative in asking for a drink, the barriers immediately go up via the woman's questions. The implication is that this encounter will be marked, like other encounters between Jew and Samaritan, by distance, disagreement and even hostility. We can even slip into a mentality where such things are not only expected but enjoyable and we resist any change to the 'status quo'. But Jesus' mission is to change the status quo, the way we like to see things however distorted they are. His response is to offer the woman another perspective on things. From this perspective ('if you only knew') she would gladly discard the barrier between them because she would see him as he truly is: a messenger from God bearing gifts ('you would have been the one to ask and he would have given you living water'). As this delightful story unfolds, the woman discovers (or is led to?) the identity of Jesus, first by a question ('are you greater than our father Jacob'?), then by a request for a share of his gift ('some of that water') and thirdly by a recognition ('you are a prophet'). This follows his 'revelation' that he knows her whole life. But Jesus' revelation of his divinely inspired insight is not done for a negative or hostile purpose (the barrier theme) but for a positive one (he identifies her as one who speaks the truth).

Now that she accepts Jesus speaks with divine authority the barrier between Jew and Samaritan can be dismantled, again by Jesus leading her to see things from another perspective ('those who worship must worship in spirit and truth'). When she professes her faith in the Messiah to come Jesus reveals his divine identity to her (*ego eimi*; 'I am'). The barrier erected in the name of religion is removed and the woman becomes a messenger of the good news to her fellow Samaritans. Jesus' disciples return and, not surprisingly, operate behind the old barrier. Jesus urges them to look again (from his perspective) and see that the barrier has gone, the Samaritans are thronging across the fields; a great harvest that 'you had not worked for'. The story ends with the report that many Samaritans believed and that Jesus stayed with them. In Christ there is no longer Jew or Samaritan; in the words of our reading from Romans 'by faith we are judged righteous and at peace with God'. The absence of peace is marked by division, its presence by communion, above all by communion with God.

Fourth Sunday of Lent

1 Samuel 16:1, 6–7, 10–13; Ephesians 5:8–14;
John 9:1–41 or 9:1, 6–9, 13–17, 34–38

The first half of John's Gospel has been well named by scholars as the 'book of signs'. Within chapters 2—12 Jesus works a number of signs that call for faith and challenge those who think they have faith. Our story of the man born blind is a particularly important and intriguing 'sign'. Jesus says of him that 'he was born blind so that the works of God might be displayed in him'. He then cures him and he becomes, in the words of some of the Pharisees, one of the 'signs like these'. But his transformation from physical blindness to sight is only part of his role as a 'sign', one in whom the works of God are displayed. What makes this story particularly important within John's Gospel is the man's journey of faith and his proclamations of faith and honesty as his story unfolds. As a model of the true disciple and a reflection of Jesus' own journey in John's Gospel, the man maintains faith and speaks the truth in a series of encounters with people who challenge him in a variety of ways—and thereby tempt him to deny or dilute faith. One could almost say that the sequence of highly condensed scenes typifies most of the 'situations' that challenge our faith.

We can imagine that the temptation to slip away from his past is quite acute when he realises that even his neighours are not sure he is the same person. But, he acknowledges that he is the one and names the man who healed him. Likewise, it would be easier to avoid trouble with the Pharisees when they ask for his opinion of Jesus by making the same answer he gave earlier when asked where Jesus was—'I do not know'. But he does not and confesses that 'he is a prophet'. According to the third scene, his family effectively abandons him and he has to face the consequences of his professions of faith all alone; the one against the many. In the fourth scene, he is surrounded by the 'Jews', the term John uses for those who, among his own people, are most hostile to Jesus and his mission. Here it is a case of the many against the one.

Another intriguing feature of this story is that, as the pressure grows on the man and he is more isolated and surrounded by 'enemies' (to use an Old Testament term), the focus on Jesus becomes more intense and the decision to remain or not remain his disciple more acute. The Jews proclaim that Jesus is a sinner; the man replies that his unique healing power is a sign that he must come from God.

Life is about decisions. Paul knows that he cannot address the details of each person's life in the church at Ephesus: to claim to do so would impinge on people's freedom. Instead he exhorts them to try and discover what is pleasing to the Lord, a process that involves making decisions. There is no avoiding this basic human reality: not to make a decision is still a decision so why try and avoid it? John's Gospel today teaches that making the right decisions about Jesus and about ourselves does not ensure an easy ride; more likely it will be the reverse. But just when we may think that our decisions, our commitments, have caused us to be completely isolated and abandoned—perhaps by those whom we love most—this Gospel story from John tells us that the one who matters most, Jesus, is with us in our isolation. When Jesus hears that they have driven the man away he finds him; he singles him out so that this story may be told about him as one in whom the works of God are displayed. He has indeed become a new man, a new creation, something that is perhaps signaled at the beginning of the story where Jesus' cure of his blindness echoes the creation of the human being from the ground in Genesis 2. Another key component of God's work in this man is that he stands as a warning to those of us who think that we see clearly but in reality are blind, our vision distorted by the kinds of things that the season of Lent invites us to tackle and assures us can be removed—like cataracts!

But, the Bible does not provide any magic way of making decisions and it tells stories where even the most graced and wise of Israel's leaders get it wrong—in good faith of course. Take the reading from 1 Samuel as an example. Samuel, one of Israel's most revered prophets, makes the wrong decision about the Lord's anointed one. In the story, God corrects him and things come to a satisfactory resolution. We will make blunders at times but as long as we are seeking for the truth and acting in honesty, we grow in faith and wisdom and the works of God are manifest in us.

Fifth Sunday of Lent

Ezekiel 37:12–14; Romans 8:8–11; John 11:1–45
or 11:3–7, 17, 20–27, 33–45

A number of themes in John's Gospel converge in the story of Jesus raising Lazarus from the dead and all we can do here is highlight some of them. Whichever way you look at this story it provides plenty of material for a homily.

This is the last sign or work in what many scholars call the 'book of signs' in the gospel (1:19 — 12:50), the sign above all that points to Jesus' passion, death and resurrection in the 'book of glory' (13:1 — 20:31). In the preceding chapter, Jesus presents himself as the good shepherd who lays down his life for his sheep (10:11–18). In chapter 11 he risks his life by going to Bethany near Jerusalem to raise his friend Lazarus from the dead. News of this miracle firms the resolve of the Jewish authorities that Jesus must die: and so he lays down his life for his sheep.

A link with the theme of glory is provided by Jesus' comment when he receives news of Lazarus's illness: he says that 'this illness does not lead to death; rather it is for God's glory so that the Son of God may be glorified through it'. There are layers of meaning embedded in this statement. It initially looks misleading because, as the story unfolds, Lazarus's illness does indeed lead to his death. But, in raising Lazarus from the dead Jesus manifests the glory of God, the one who has power over life and death. This will be manifested fully in the death and resurrection of Jesus himself.

But there is more. As already noted, the act of raising Lazarus leads to Jesus' own death in being raised on the cross. Paradoxically, this repulsive death will become the great sign of God's love for the world and will 'draw all people to myself' (12:32) because 'the ruler of this world will be driven out'. The revelation of God's saving purpose for humanity is the glory of God and in this God's son is also glorified. The victory over death is not primarily over physical death but the 'real death' that the world suffers from because of its enslavement to the powers of this world that are exposed in the 'sin of the world'.

This connection between the story of Lazarus and the passion, death and resurrection of Jesus ushers in another important theme, the massive difference between resuscitation and resurrection.[1] Lazarus is raised back to life in this world and will die again like any mortal; resurrection is a rising to eternal life free of the powers of death that disfigure and demean our human life. In the story this difference is expressed in two ways. One is via the exchange between Jesus and Martha that climaxes with Jesus' proclamation 'I am the resurrection'. The other is the dramatic way in which Lazarus comes forth from the tomb bound hand and foot in the shrouds of death and has to be released. In contrast, when the disciples discover the empty tomb on Easter morning, the shrouds of death are found rolled up and in their place, a sign that the one who was wrapped in them has, without any evidence of a struggle, freed himself from the bonds of death.

Granted that this is a fair reading of the story, there is a danger that this line of thinking demeans the drama and disaster of Lazarus's illness and death—in short the dissolution that is our physical end. It merely provides a setting, an occasion for the key proclamation about Jesus' glorification. However, as I read the story, the evangelist is well aware of this danger and deftly counters it by the way he portrays Jesus' involvement in Lazarus' death and the mourning that accompanies it. The death of this friend and the grief of his sisters move Jesus deeply to grieve with them. One commentator notes that men in those times did not normally weep at a death; this was the role of women. Jesus' break with custom is a manifestation of his solidarity and sympathy with the bereaved.[2] In theological terms, we might also say the story is subtly combining the notions of transcendence and immanence. The transcendent one, the Son of God, is able to enter fully into the profound sorrow and loss that human beings feel at the death of a loved one. If this is the case with Lazarus, then it is also the case with each human life. And if the life and death of Lazarus is the locus of a manifestation of the glory of Jesus and the Father, then so must it also be with the life and death of each one of us, only more so because our death leads not to resuscitation but resurrection.

---

1. In an apparent oversight, the New Jerusalem Bible introduces our story with the heading 'The Resurrection of Lazarus'!
2. Cf Teresa Okure's comment in her commentary on John's Gospel in *The International Bible Commentary* (Collegeville: The Liturgical Press, 1998) 1482.

Palm Sunday of the Passion

Isaiah 50:4–7; Philippians 2:6–11;
Matthew 26:14–27:66 or 27:11–54

Matthew's account of Jesus' passion and death is marked at strategic points by references to the fulfillment of the Scriptures. This is in keeping with the rest of the gospel, in particular the account of Jesus' birth with which the gospel begins. The account commences with the report that Judas betrayed him for thirty pieces of silver: when Judas returns the money later, prompting the priests to buy the potter's field, we learn that this is in fulfillment of a prophecy in the book of Jeremiah. Jesus foretells that his disciples will abandon him, again in fulfillment of the Scriptures. Peter and the disciples proclaim (sic prophesy) that they will never abandon Jesus but their prophecy has only human backing and fails 'to be fulfilled'. Their desertion of Jesus reveals the emptiness of prophecies that do not come from God. How often do we human beings make grand predictions and prophecies about ourselves and our world, only to see the emptiness of them in due course.

Again, when Jesus is arrested in the garden, he appeals to the Scriptures to forbid the use of violence on his behalf. The way of the cross, the way of non-violence in the face of violence, is the way of God and it fulfills the Scriptures. This amounts to a massive claim in relation to some violent Old Testament texts such as in the book of Joshua (Hebrew for 'saviour'). The servant passages in the book of Isaiah show that ancient Israelites differed in their understanding of how God triumphs over evil and oppression. The fact that these differing views are present in the Bible suggests that those who put the final product together thought it wise to include them for our reflection rather than adjudicate between them.

In the trial scene before the high priest, the key issue is the truth and authority of Jesus' own prophecies. False witnesses are paraded to accuse the true prophet of false and blasphemous prophecies. In response, Jesus prophesies that they will see the fulfillment of his prophecy about the exaltation of the 'Son of Man'. The scene ends dramatically with Jesus being mocked as a prophet. Such disputes about prophecy and its fulfillment are not so appropriate in the trial before Pilate, a pagan. In their place, Matthew portrays Jesus as fulfilling the prophecy of the suffering servant of Isaiah 52:13—53:12 who remains silent before his accusers. Jesus' silence amazes Pilate, in fulfillment of the prophecy in Isaiah that nations and kings will be amazed and reduced to silence before the servant. Finally, on the cross Jesus invokes the opening words of the famous Psalm 22, 'my God, my God, why have you forsaken me?' Jesus is one with all those who cry out in lament to God from a situation of powerlessness and oppression. The one who can enter so completely into the situation of lament is the one who can rescue us from our lamentable situations (the fulfillment of the prayer of lament).

Why this focus on the fulfillment of Scripture? No doubt there is more than one reason but surely an important one is to signal that Jesus' passion and death is more than what it appears to be on the surface—the result of hostility, intrigue, fear and violence. Rather, it is the high point of God's purpose for humanity and the Scriptures (both the Old Testament and Jesus' own words) testify that God's purpose is salvation. The astonishing thing is that even those who betray Jesus (Judah, Peter), those who fail him (the disciples), those who mock him (the priests, the crowds), and the pagans who sentence him to a violent death (Pilate) are all mysteriously embraced within God's overall saving purpose, as are all those who preceded this moment and all those who follow this moment (who will see the Son of Man seated at the right hand of Power).

Matthew's account points to the presence of God's saving purpose by also presenting a number of unlikely or unexpected people who step forward to testify to the truth of Jesus and what is taking place. There is the contrast between those who, at the beginning of the narrative, hand Jesus over to his executioners (Judas, the disciples who abandon him, Peter who denies him) and Joseph of Arimathea, to whom the body of Jesus is handed over by the executioners. Matthew's brief report even allows one to think that Joseph has become a disciple because of, or in the wake of, Jesus' death. The disciples who fail to keep vigil with Jesus in the garden are 'fulfilled' by women disciples at the end of the account who keep vigil at the cross and at the tomb. Judas proclaims that he is a sinner who has offended against 'innocent blood'. The truth of his confession and testimony highlights the bogus testimony of the clergy. Pilate dissembles under pressure from the crowd as his wife sends her clear message that Jesus is an innocent man. Finally, whereas the crowd mocks Jesus' identity as 'God's Son', the centurion confesses 'Truly, this man was God's Son'. The crowd does not grasp what is taking place on their behalf but the centurion does and so does the earth which trembles at what is a cosmic event. A striking feature of the crucifixion scene is the sign *on* the cross, 'This is Jesus, the king of the Jews'. The sign *of* the cross turns these words into a prophecy and fulfills them in a way that their authors (not named in Matthew) could never envisage.

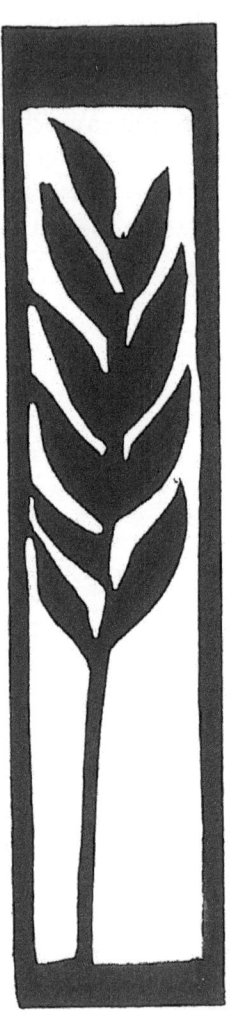

Thursday in Holy Week

Exodus 12:1–8, 11–14; 1 Corinthians 11:23–26; John 13:1–15

Feet may not have all that much symbolic value in our contemporary culture and liturgy; we tend to focus on hands (joined in prayer), lips (singing praise), ears (hearing the word), and so on. But feet were a highly valued symbol of royal and divine power in ancient times. A victorious leader would tread on the prone bodies of his enemies (Josh 10:24); the ark of the covenant evoked the footstool on which the enthroned Lord of hosts rested 'his feet'; the fleet of foot messenger was crucial for getting messages to their destination (for example, news of the outcome of a battle). Washing a guest's feet on entering a house was a sign of welcome and hospitality. No doubt part of the reason for the value accorded feet in the ancient world was because walking was how one generally got around. Mechanised transport has caused us to lose sight of our feet, so to speak.

In contrast, the Gospel of John has a profound appreciation of the symbolic significance of feet and outlines it in three passages about foot washing: Mary's anointing of the feet of Jesus in John 12, Jesus' washing of the feet of his disciples at the last supper, and his instruction that they should do the same to one another. In John's Gospel, the anointing of Jesus' feet by Mary marks the end of his preaching mission. His evening with Martha, Mary and Lazarus is the final stopover before his entry into Jerusalem where his glorification and 'return' to the Father will take place. Tired, dirty, calloused feet are the mark of the committed preacher, a sign of total giving, and Jesus gave himself completely to his preaching mission, trudging ceaselessly around Palestine. It is also a sign of his love for those who are troubled or in need, and the anointing of his feet by Mary acknowledges this. Jesus had recently raised her brother Lazarus from the dead. This self-giving that marks Jesus' preaching journeys will reach its fulfillment in his death on the cross, as Jesus intimates in his reply to Judas who objects to the use of expensive ointment to wash feet.

In washing the feet of his disciples during the last supper Jesus, like Mary, expresses his love and appreciation of his disciples who accompanied him throughout his many journeys. But, more importantly, one may say that now, as he prepares to 'return' to the Father, he 'anoints' their feet to carry forward his mission of preaching the Good News of salvation to the whole world. In a symbolic sense, their feet become Christ's feet and their footsteps his footsteps. He now works through them: as Paul says in Romans 10:15 'how will there be preachers if they are not sent? As Scripture says: How beautiful are the feet of the messenger of good news'. Calloused, dirty, tired but, in the service of Christ, transformed into beautiful feet!

But what is more, the disciples are to become Christ to each other and this is encapsulated in Jesus' instruction that they are to wash each other's feet. In a powerful symbolic gesture but one that is somewhat foreign to us, what they do to each other's feet will be a sign of how they love one another. And, like Jesus who washed the feet of all the disciples, Judas and those who would betray and abandon him, so they are to love one another whether good or bad. As the words of Jesus make clear ('not all of your are clean'), this does not mean turning a blind eye to evil; what it does mean is extending the mercy of God towards all and sundry, even in the face of rejection.

In relation to this it is significant that the disciples are all washed with the one bowl and the same water. In years gone by a mother would normally run only one bath for several of her children to wash in; not the kind of thing we do nowadays (I would guess that in most of our Holy Thursday liturgies we would pour fresh water from a jug for each participant's foot rather than do as Jesus did). It is also significant that John uses the broader term 'disciples' and not the more restricted 'the twelve': we are not told how many feet Jesus washed. In an intriguing way, the text is somewhat open-ended.

While it is nice to have the foot-washing in our Holy Thursday liturgy, the challenge embedded in it is quite beyond us. We can only respond to it by being remade in the image and likeness of Christ. Jesus comes to us in the Eucharist to do just this. In the words of St Augustine: 'I am your food, but instead of my being transformed into you, it is you who shall be transformed into me'.

Good Friday

*Isaiah 52:13—53:12; Hebrews 4:14–16; 5:7–9;
John 18:1—19:42*

The Jewish authorities may have seen Jesus' execution as the elimination of a messianic fraud, while the Romans probably saw it as an opportunity to remove a potential troublemaker. However, the resurrection of Jesus and the linking of this with his whole life and ministry rendered any such explanations of his death completely false for the church community. To answer the question why did he die the way he did, they turned to the two great ideas or images of God that course through the Bible: the just judge who is rightly intolerant of evil and the merciful lover who forgives. It is difficult for us to harmonise these powerful and dynamic images, and the point may be that we are not meant to in this life, but they provide a crucial context for giving meaning to the life of faith. A brief review of some major attempts to answer the question 'why' will illustrate this.

One quite influential line of thought was that, by his death, Jesus paid the penalty for the sins of the world. It was beyond the ability or power of any human being to do so because, being flawed, any human action no matter how good would still be imperfect and inadequate. Only the 'Son of God', Jesus, both God and man, could satisfy the divine demand for justice.

This explanation attempts to give due weight to the theology of a just God but ends up with a somewhat bizarre image of God. If God would not forgive us our sins until his Son satisfied him by dying on the cross then God is even less forgiving than many human beings. If we feel that we are somehow compensated for an offence by the satisfaction of watching the guilty party suffer, we are being pretty vengeful and, many would say, infantile. *A fortiori* it reveals an infantile theology of God. Despite its odd logic, this idea has been popular, perhaps because it touches a vengeful chord in us. We create God in our own image and likeness.

Another explanation, and one that surfaces at times in the liturgy, is that Jesus suffered as the representative of the human race; he suffered *instead* of the human race, and his suffering was a kind of ransom paid to the devil in order to free sinners who had sold their souls to the devil. It does convey the notion of a heroic figure who hands himself over to the enemy to free the prisoners. But, how can God or Jesus be beholden to the devil in any form? The notion of God paying a ransom to the devil in some kind of just transaction looks quite odd.

These answers to why Jesus died pay due attention to the seriousness of sin but fail to pay due attention to the theology of God as merciful lover. Love of course is meant here in its biblical meaning of God's commitment and loyalty to us. As the Gospel of John puts it, God wants to take away the sin of the world and restore to its full glory the relationship between God and humanity. For us poor human beings to experience this and to make a free decision in response to God's initiative (if not free then it is not a fully human decision), this restoration needs to take place in the human realm, in a human way. God's commitment to bringing this about is revealed in the incarnation of his Son who carries out the will of the Father—as such this is a perfect act of love between the Father and the Son, as well a perfect act of love of human beings for whom the Son becomes flesh and gives himself completely.

On this understanding, Jesus' death on the cross was not something necessary, ordained by God, that he had to endure. It was the Roman method of crucifixion for criminals at that time. What was necessary was that when Jesus was confronted with rejection and hatred—the absence of love—he continued to love unconditionally, even those who set out to kill him by crucifying him. As has been said by many Christians throughout the centuries reflecting on Jesus and his life: being fully human and loving others unconditionally will almost inevitably get you killed. In this sense, one can say that death for Jesus was inevitable because of what he stood for, preached about, and lived. The life of love that culminated in his death is for all of us who cannot love like this and, in the mysterious operation of God's grace, embraces and empowers us to become like Jesus and love like him.

Where is the justice component in all this? May I suggest that Jesus' act of perfect love is perfectly just: it is not done for any other motive than love of the Father (obedience to the Father's will) and love of wounded humanity. The biblical notion of justice/righteousness is a proper relationship and complete loyalty to that relationship. The just judge is one who is always loyal to right relationships in society; always delivering people from the threat of injustice.

The theologian Herbert McCabe notes that from one point of view the cross is the sacrament of the sin of the world—it is the sign of the ultimate sin that was made inevitable by the kind of world that we human beings have made. From another point of view it is the sacrament of our forgiveness, because it is the ultimate sign of God's love for us.[3] As Psalm 63 says, 'your love Lord, is better than life'.

---

3. Cf Herbert McCabe, *God Matters* (London: Continuum, 2005 [reprint]), 98.

Easter

*Genesis 1:1—2:2 or 1:1, 26–31; Genesis 22:1–18;
Exodus 14:15—15:1; Isaiah 54:5–14; Isaiah 55:1–11;
Baruch 3:9–15, 3:32—4:4; Ezekiel 36:16–17a, 18–28
Romans 6:3–11; Matthew 28:1–10*

As one listens to the series of Old Testament readings during the Easter vigil, one could be forgiven for thinking that God has an almighty ego. When Abraham passes God's 'test' of detachment from his son Isaac, God does not say 'blessed are you Abraham' but 'now I know you fear God'. According to the reading from Exodus, the whole purpose of the deliverance at the sea is that the Egyptians and Israel 'will learn that I am the Lord'. There is no let up in the subsequent readings either. According to the two passages from Isaiah, the Lord is 'called the God of all the earth', and nations will come streaming to Israel not for its sake but 'for the sake of the Lord your God'. The reading from Ezekiel is even more strident.

Perhaps a clue to God's unswerving resolve to be acknowledged by all lies in the first reading from Genesis, which claims that the human being is made in the image and likeness of God. The implication of this claim, when read in conjunction with the subsequent readings, is that we will only be able to live in the image and likeness of God when we know who God is. Hence the Bible expends a lot of text telling its readers about God's name and nature, as well as identifying false images of God and false gods. For Christians, Jesus is the perfect image and likeness of God who has come on earth to show us how we can become like him. The way Jesus reveals God is a surprising and even shocking one, particularly when one thinks of the crucifixion as an image and likeness of God. Perhaps this shows just how mysterious God is and how little we know, particularly when we think we know. In a sense, it justifies the Old Testament harping on our need to 'know that I am the Lord' and correcting false knowledge.

With the grace of God we can come to see that the crucifixion is a revelation of the nature of God because the crucified one is the resurrected one. The perfect image and likeness of God bears the marks of his suffering and death in his glorified body. These thoughts can provide some background as we now turn to reflect on the gospel accounts of the resurrection.

Matthew's account begins dramatically: an earthquake, an angel descending from heaven with a face like lightning, rolling the tombstone away. And in contrast, the frightened soldiers 'like dead men'. As I read Matthew, a key feature is contrast; the contrast between the world of dead men (the world without the resurrection) and the divine, life–giving world that irrupts into it.

Recall the last part of Matthew's account of the passion. The Jewish authorities request soldiers to guard the tomb of the dead Jesus and Pilate grants their request. They seek to extend into the realm of death the control that they exercised over Jesus during his trial and crucifixion. Such obsession with control over another person reveals a deep unease about whether one is actually in control. The tomb captures the ambiguous and fraught nature of their perceptions nicely. On the one hand it is a place of darkness, of no movement, of silence and so no threat to those outside. On the other hand it has to be barricaded and guarded as if there is a real threat to those outside. Ambiguity and illusions of control are swept aside by the angel who, with a blazing face and great power, rolls the stone effortlessly away. The real place of darkness, of silence and fear is revealed as the world in which people like the Jewish authorities and the soldiers live 'like dead men'. But the angel is no threat to them, instead of rushing at them as enemies, he sits on the tombstone and speaks to the women: his first words are 'do not fear . . . he has risen'.

The women themselves are under the fear instilling control of the authorities: they can only approach the tomb with the permission of the guard. The new guard's word is liberating and empowering. They are now sent as angels (= messengers in Greek) to bear the good news of the resurrection to the disciples. They are no longer guarded but sent in freedom and trust. But fear runs deep in human beings and it is not all eradicated in a moment. Matthew seems to remind us of this when he says that they went away 'in fear and great joy'. Joy is gaining the upper hand but fear still lingers, perhaps a different kind of fear to the one with which they approached the tomb. A further transformation is needed and it comes in the encounter with Jesus 'coming to meet them'. Like the angel, he greets them with the words 'do not fear'.

Their encounter with Jesus is transforming because he himself has been transformed in the resurrection. The one who was rejected by men, degraded and disfigured through his scourging, crowning with thorns and crucifixion, is now revealed as someone to be embraced and adored, the very image and likeness of God. This transformation is reflected in the tradition of Christian art where one of the most repulsive forms of human torture and death, the cross, is transformed into a most treasured and desirable sign of God and God's love for us.

It is the encounter with Jesus that banishes any lingering fear from the women. They are now sisters of their risen brother Jesus and can bear a message of hope and reconciliation to his estranged brothers, the disciples: 'tell my brothers that they must leave for Galilee; they will see me there'. Our faith in the resurrection depends on the message of these women, filled with the joy and grace of their encounter with the risen Christ. Generations through the centuries have emulated their mission and it is largely because of their fidelity that we too can be transformed like them into angels of God's good news.

People of course must be free to accept or reject the message. But for those weighing the options I think Matthew's account invites us to consider two things.

1. If we reject the resurrection, do we do so openly and honestly, or are we mounting close guard at the door of our heart so that nothing goes in and nothing comes out that we do not have control over? Do we want to be like an angel or a corpse, the walking dead?

2. If we claim to believe in the resurrection, can we live it in our earthly life, as the disciples were called to do? Can we see and celebrate goodness, beauty and desirability in the pain, suffering and disfigurement of others? Can we see and embrace Christ in our suffering humanity, or accept the embrace of those who see us as suffering humanity? Like Catherine of Siena who used to embrace and kiss those to whom she ministered; covered as they were in sores.

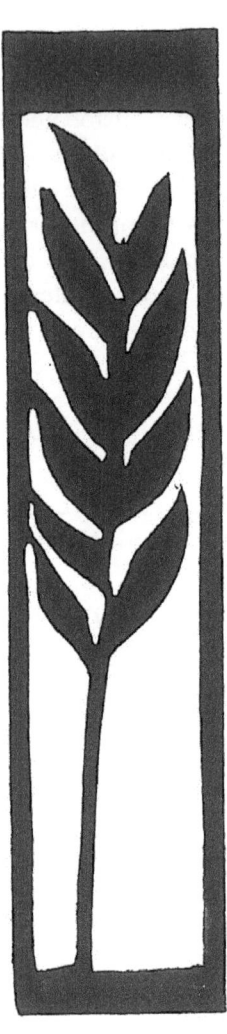

Second Sunday of Easter

Acts 2:42–47; 1 Peter 1:3–9; John 20:19–31

The text from Acts portrays the peace and harmony of the early post-Easter community; a reality that lasts, one might say, only a few verses. Pretty soon there are persecutions, problems within the community (the episode of Ananias and Sapphira), the debate over the Gentiles, and so on. The passage from 1 Peter reflects something of this at times painful growth of the early church, of having 'to bear being plagued by all sorts of trials'. As we read these texts in our post-Easter setting, it is important to keep the passage from Acts in mind. By describing what we might call an ideal situation it makes the claim that the promises of Jesus are not 'pie in the sky' romance. They are part of the church's experience. A similar move can be seen in 1 Kings 3—8 which claims that the promises of Deuteronomy were realised, if only briefly, in the reign of Solomon. Various factors can intrude to trouble peace and harmony in the community: sin and strife within, persecution from without, an unforeseen disaster. But the memory of the ideal that was experienced fuels faith and hope that it can be realised again—each time of course in its own unique way, a way that meets the times and needs of the particular community.

The letter of 1 Peter reminds us of the faith, hope and love that are the remedy for the pain of trials and tribulations. The passage from John's Gospel, the famous encounter between doubting Thomas and the risen Jesus, provides us with a model of how to handle one of the most challenging 'trials' that the church community can face—the refusal to believe in the resurrection. The way Jesus responds to a genuine doubter like Thomas, not with condemnation and excommunication, but with a genuine concern to meet and help him overcome his difficulties, is something for us to emulate as best we can in our world where faith is such a fraught issue. As I see it, it is not so much a question of faith (religion) or no–faith (secularism and/or atheism). Human beings always need to believe in someone or something: rather it is a question of what kind of faith will fire peoples' lives and give them meaning. An atheist believes there is no God but can no more prove this than I can prove there is a God.

Here again the letter of 1 Peter offers some rich reflection on those three central virtues by which human beings live and find meaning in their lives—faith, hope and love. One could almost imagine that the author of this letter had been reading Paul's great discourse in 1 Corinthians 13. According to 1 Peter, faith in the resurrection of Jesus is accompanied by 'a new birth as his sons'. This new birth will reach its fulfillment in our resurrection from the dead when we will share fully in the resurrection of Jesus. This faith in turns fuels our hope and enables us to bear all kinds of trials. We have 'a sure hope and the promise of an inheritance that can never be spoilt'. While our hope is fueled by our faith that we will share fully in the resurrection of Jesus, there is more to it than this. The letter speaks of 'the salvation' to be revealed at the end of time; not just my salvation. Our faith and hope in the resurrection cannot therefore be separated from this general salvation; a measure of our faith and hope is our commitment to this universal cause.

But one can only believe and hope in another whom one loves. We are reluctant to trust people with whom we are in conflict and we don't expect anything from them. Christian love enables us to overcome both these barriers but we are only able to become Christian lovers because God first loved us. Such is the bond between faith, hope and love that we are able, as the letter states, to love Jesus even though we have not seen him. What is more—and here 1 Peter goes beyond Paul's discourse in 1 Corinthians—this bond of faith, hope and love fills us with joy. This does not mean that I am always on a high; joy here is one of the gifts that flow from faith in the resurrection; it is the conviction of being deeply loved, a certain serenity that enables one to endure the most severe trials, the ones that seek to induce fear and anxiety. The love of Jesus is a power that guards our life. Faith, hope, love and joy: these are the same 'ingredients' that filled the community in Acts. They are in us and shine through in various ways both in our community and individual lives—a manifestation of the resurrection.

Third Sunday of Easter

Acts 2:14, 22–28; 1 Peter 1:17–21 Luke 24:13–35

The hope of the two men on the road to Emmaus was that Jesus would set Israel free. Luke does not specify just what freedom they had in mind but more than likely it was about Israel's freedom from the Roman yoke, leading to the reestablishment of the Israelite state. But the freedom that Jesus brings is something at once more particular and more universal. It is freedom from the yoke of sin that troubles everyone, whether Jew or Gentile, and that turns us into oppressors driven by fear of the other. In order to be free, we need to 'see' our liberator and the kind of liberation that he brings. Luke's wonderful story of the disciples on the road to Emmaus unfolds key stages in this liberating experience.

The story begins in a way that reminds one of the defeat of a cause: the former community of believers is now fragmented and leaving Jerusalem, the scene of Jesus' brutal end. The two disciples are no doubt part of a much larger group that had followed him to Jerusalem—Lk 29:37 speaks of a whole multitude. They now return home in dribs and drabs. There is a sense that it is all past tense ('our hope had been', but not any more). Jesus seeks out those trapped in hopelessness.

The women's report that angels have told them Jesus is alive has astounded them (NRSV; the verb can mean 'disturb') but not changed them. Why? A clue is that there is no report of anyone seeing Jesus 'alive'. The disciples, both those in Jerusalem and those on the way, think of resuscitation not resurrection; it would mean that Jesus has in some way cheated death and come back to them again. We take the doctrine of the resurrection so much for granted that we tend to forget what a revolution in thinking it really is. Perhaps we, like them, tend to think of it in some sense 'like' resuscitation. To grasp something of the resurrection, one's horizons need to be transformed; the revelation that is the resurrection is itself a liberation, an opening of our eyes by God.

How are the eyes of faithful yet blind disciples to be opened? We all think within a context and these men have been operating within the context of their understanding of the Scriptures (for them of course the Old Testament) and how they linked Jesus, 'a great prophet', to the great prophets of the Scriptures. Jesus challenges them to look at the Scriptures again, this time through his eyes, and see that the passage of the Christ through suffering and death to glory is in reality the fulfillment of the Scriptures. In fulfilling the Scriptures Jesus transforms their meaning: the claim of the gospel is that he is the only one who can reveal the full meaning of the Scriptures.

The climactic moment of freedom from hopelessness, from a reluctance to believe the message of the women, from a limited understanding of Scripture, comes in the breaking of the bread. It is well recognised that Luke is here alluding to the Eucharist. As the breaking of the bread in this story is the moment when the resurrected one reveals himself by 'opening their eyes', so the presence of the Lord Jesus is 'revealed' to the eyes of faith in the Eucharist. It is the same Christ who suffered, died and entered into glory who is present to the disciples on the way to Emmaus and to any community celebrating the Eucharist.

The final scene in this story touches a central aspect of the freedom that Jesus brings—the freedom from sin in all its forms. In a sign of the reestablishment of the fragmented community of Jesus, the two disciples return to the others in Jerusalem and there are told that Jesus 'has risen and has appeared to Simon'. Note the change in terminology from the disciples' earlier words about Jesus being reported to be 'alive' to 'he has risen'. A transformation of faith has occurred; the past is seen in a new light and in being seen in this way it can be embraced with all its faults and failings. But the point that particularly strikes me in the context of Luke's Gospel is the focus here on Simon/Peter. Luke alone of the Evangelists reports how, after Peter had denied his Lord three times, Jesus turned and looked at him. Peter turned away and wept. Jesus has now come to free Peter from a burden too heavy to bear: the realisation that he had betrayed his saviour.

Fourth Sunday of Easter

Acts 2:14, 36–41; 1 Peter 2:20–25; John 10:1–10

The first part of John's Gospel in today's readings is a pretty complex parable with a number of players: there are the thieves and brigands, the shepherd, the gatekeeper, the sheep, the stranger(s). Then there is the gate of the sheepfold. The subsequent explanation of the parable, triggered by the disciples' failure to understand, springs a surprise by focusing on something unexpected—the gate—before moving to the focus that we were probably expecting—the shepherd. The shift to the shepherd is signaled in the last verse of our reading ('I have come') and is developed more fully in verses 11–16.

If this parable is anything to go by, running a sheep farm in those days seems to have been a rather risky business. The sheep need to be penned in because of the threat of thieves, there is need for a guard (the gatekeeper), the shepherd has to single out his sheep by name, presumably so that he does not make off with any that are not his. The sheep themselves have to be pretty smart, at least in this parable, knowing the voice of their shepherd and their own names. We tend to have a warm trusting image of a shepherd and this no doubt owes much to the image of Jesus as the Good Shepherd and to famous psalms such as Psalm 23. But there is evidence, as our parable implies, that shepherds in the ancient world were a mix of good and bad. It was not regarded highly as a way of life (partly no doubt because of the dangers) and so the task often fell to those on the fringes of society. At certain times, settled societies complained of 'shepherd tribes' who were notorious as robbers. As so often, the Bible takes an ambiguous or even despised image (*cf* the cross) and shows how it can be transformed it into something that reveals the presence of God.

The metaphor of Jesus as a gate is surprising to the modern mind and difficult to appreciate, at least at first glance. We instinctively prefer the gatekeeper, the sheep, the thieves and brigands. Many have thought the gatekeeper to be the Father or the Holy Spirit, while the thieves and brigands are the Jewish authorities who are portrayed in the gospel as hostile to Jesus and his disciples and who, according to John 8:44, have the devil as their father. There may be something in these speculations but it is significant that neither the gatekeeper nor the thieves are identified in this passage: perhaps this is to focus attention on the gate and the sheep. And while a gate may not look a very engaging metaphor for a person, the Bible is adept at taking what looks to be unpromising and transforming it.

The parable and the explanation of the gate and the shepherd may be summed up in the statement from next Sunday's gospel where Jesus says, 'I am the way, and the truth, and the life. No one comes to the Father except through me.' There is only one way, one gate, to life or salvation and it is Jesus. One has the impression that, in the parable and its explanation of the gate, the thieves and brigands are exposed as such because they try to enter the sheepfold by another gate. But there is only one way in and out and the sheep recognise this. Why are they able to recognise this truth from falsehood? Because this gate is not just any gate to a place where sheep are locked up for fear of marauders. In a characteristic biblical move, the static, somewhat forbidding image of a gate guarding a threatened sheepfold is transformed into a kind of 'arch of freedom' through which sheep move from pasture to pasture. In fact, by the end of our reading the image of a gate has been so transformed that it begins to disappear and be replaced by, or blend into, the image of Jesus as the Shepherd. Jesus as the gate opens the way to Jesus as the Shepherd.

No doubt this gospel parable has been located within the liturgy of the Easter season because of its emphasis on life and deliverance from enemies. Also, no doubt, because disciples are called to continue the work of their resurrected Lord by being shepherds of the flock. But a shepherd can turn into a thief, like the ones Jesus condemns. How to avoid this? One way, so the gospel suggests, is to listen to the sheep. They recognise the voice of their Master and will not listen to the voice of thieves and brigands.

A mistake in reading the gospel passage would be to think that one can know who the sheep are. True, they are the ones who listen to the shepherd's voice but it is the shepherd who knows them even before this. The reading from Acts reminds the Shepherd's disciples that the invitation should be made to all outsiders no matter who they are or where they come from or what they may have done beforehand. The reading from 1 Peter reminds us in its turn that we are all 'one flock' in that we are all freed by Jesus from the burden of sin and guilt.

Fifth Sunday of Easter

Acts 6:1–7; 1 Peter 2:4–9 John 14:1–12

The building industry should be happy this Sunday (and last Sunday as well); metaphors drawn from their world are to the fore—stones, houses, rooms, etc. All metaphors are limited and although these ones evoke powerful impressions of home, security and permanence, they can appear static, lacking dynamism. The letter of 1 Peter is well aware of this and speaks of 'living stones' in the process of being built into a 'spiritual house'. Construction is going on all the time. A building needs sure foundations and the letter claims that it has the best because Christ is the corner stone. This faith claim is supported by appeal to a number of Old Testament texts that also employ building metaphors. Jesus is the stone to which they refer, the key structural element in the new Zion that is the Christian community.

The reading from Acts provides an example of the kind of dynamic construction that 1 Peter has in mind. The growth of the church creates a problem between Hellenist and Hebrew members. It is resolved by the appointment of seven deacons and the church continues to grow. These new 'living stones' become an integral part of the building, as integral as the apostles who anoint them. As well, they provide a structure or space within this spiritual house where both Hellenists and Hebrews can find their home.

What is the purpose of this spiritual house that is under construction? Two things, and their order is important. The first is to 'offer spiritual sacrifices acceptable to God'. The Christian community must above all be a focus of the worship of God, celebrating God's presence in its midst. The second flows from this: 'to proclaim the mighty acts of him who called you'. The Christian community invites all others to join its household and its worship of God in Jesus Christ.

One might think that 1 Peter is about the church on earth whereas the gospel reading is about heaven where Jesus has gone to prepare a place for us. In a sense this is true but there is more to it than this and it unfolds in the discourse between Jesus and his disciples. As is characteristic of John's Gospel, questions from puzzled disciples allow Jesus to expand their limited human horizons and in faith 'see' divine realities. Thomas is first up with his question about knowing the way to the Father's dwelling. He takes literally Jesus' statement about going 'to prepare a place for you' and returning; he wants a kind of road map. He wants to find his own way there, an indication that he does not fully trust Jesus as guide. In reply Jesus tells Thomas that 'I am the way, and the truth and the life'. Jesus is the 'way' to the Father, the only one through whom access to the Father and the Father's dwelling can be gained. One needs to place complete trust in him. But there is more in the metaphors of the way and the house to unfold. The trigger is provided by the next question, this time from Philip. He presumes that Jesus can point out the Father as one human being would point out another. But this kind of spatial separation of one from another does not operate in the Godhead. The Father dwells in Jesus as Jesus dwells in the Father. One enters via the 'gate' that is Jesus to find in him the dwelling place of the Father, the heavenly mansion with its many rooms. Here as elsewhere in John, the text moves smoothly from the metaphors to the reality to which they point: the mysterious indwelling of the Father and the Son.

Because of this indwelling, the works that Jesus does are the works of the Father. In an extraordinary move, the final part of our gospel claims that the disciple will, like Jesus, do the works of the Father. For this to be so, the disciples must share in the indwelling between Father and Son. Furthermore, Jesus promises that disciples will do even greater works than him. How can this be so? Perhaps it is because the disciples will be instruments in bringing about the fulfillment of what Jesus has begun in his earthly life: the salvation of the world.

All metaphors and images are limited; this Sunday's examples may not appeal to everyone as a symbol of the church community. Some may prefer the metaphor of the vine and its branches or the shepherd and the sheep or the simile of the wedding feast. The Bible provides a rich variety of images so that one can choose what is appropriate for a particular situation—all the time of course, recognizing its limitations by keeping the larger context of other images in mind. Thus the metaphor of the way can create a sense of distance from God and Jesus counters this by pointing to himself as the way. Similarly, the metaphor of a house can create a sense of something elsewhere than here (note how we travel to holiday resorts in another place) and the letter of Peter counters this by pointing to the readers/listeners as God's house, 'living stones'.

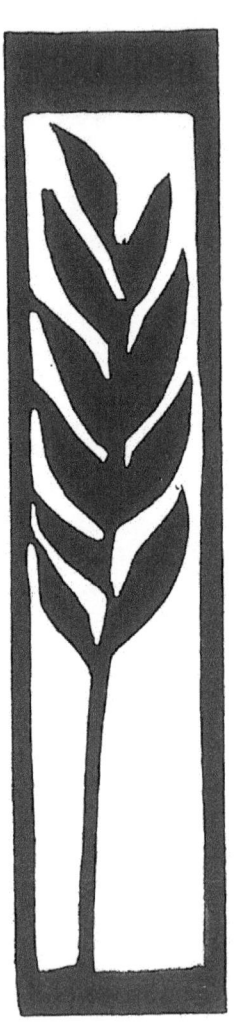

Sixth Sunday of Easter

Acts 8:5–8, 14–17; 1 Peter 3:15–18; John 14:15–21

If last Sunday's Gospel reading from John (14:1–12) emphasises the need to trust/have faith in Jesus, this Sunday's reading emphasises love. The promise of an advocate/paraclete completes the well-known trio of faith, hope and love. These are the three virtues or values by which I believe all human beings find meaning in their lives, whether they are theists or atheists (an atheist believes there is no god and so has faith). Christianity claims that believers are infused with these 'theological virtues' and, according to the principle that grace perfects nature, they inform and perfect human faith, hope and love.

We can link the three readings as follows: the gospel is about the life of the community, in particular its relationship with Jesus and the Father. It is important that this relationship, based on faith, hope and love, be secured before Jesus goes to the Father. The readings from Acts and 1 Peter are about the mission of the community. The gospel reading begins and ends with the statement that those who love Jesus will keep (hold fast to) his commandments. Obedience to Jesus' commands such as 'love one another as I have loved you' is not a way of gaining his or the Father's love. Quite the reverse. We can only love because God has first loved us (God so loved the world that he sent his only Son). Hence, keeping the commandments is an expression of our love for the one who loves us. The commandments also provide a 'way' whereby we can love others as Jesus loves them and loves us. It hardly needs to be said that the biblical notion of love is not the same as the modern western romantic idea. Rather, it means loyalty and commitment. This is not the kind of loyalty that, say, binds members of a sporting club in rivalry with 'other' clubs. It is a giving of oneself for others, a sharing of one's life, of all that one has. And so

Jesus promises us that his closest 'colleague', an advocate with impeccable credentials, will work tirelessly on our behalf forever.

All this talk of Jesus being with us forever, of an advocate to advise and guide us, of sharing life fully with the Father and the Son, as well as with other members of the community, poses quite a challenge for Christianity in the modern world, obsessed with individualism, personal space, and freedom. Many might feel that it is all too close, too overwhelming and a threat to one's freedom. On top of this there is the call to keep commandments—this surely rules out personal freedom! But our faith claims that it is precisely the presence of Jesus in one's life, of the advocate, of the Father, of obedience to the commands of love, that makes one a full and free individual. What is the basis of this claim? Surely, Jesus himself who, it is difficult even for an atheist to deny, was a supremely free human being. Yet, he obeyed the Father in all things. If we believe this message (faith) and live it in complete loyalty (love), then we are assured that we will become what we really desire to be—fully human (hope), as those weak-kneed disciples, trapped by fear, became free to live and proclaim the gospel.

Another difficulty or temptation that can arise in the modern individualistic world is that I cannot see beyond my 'personal relationship' with Jesus who dwells in me. In effect I become a consumer, oblivious of the other and resentful of anything that disturbs my self-absorption. But one cannot become fully human in the Christian sense without, like Jesus, being for others and sharing divine life with others. The reading from Acts tells how the preaching of the Good News forges a new community of those who believe it, freeing it from the divisions caused by unclean spirits, possession, and illness. More importantly, it removes the age-old barrier between Samaritans and Jews. The reading from 1 Peter provides advice on how to respond to those who challenge the values by which a Christian lives (here hope is singled out) or those who persecute one for living by such values. Whether we encounter those who welcome the message or are hostile to it, the principle that guides our actions is the same—the example of Jesus. So we should even be willing to endure the persecution of others for their sake, for their salvation, because a key principle by which we as Christians live is that Christ has done the same for us so that we might enjoy life to the full.

Ascension of the Lord

Acts 1:1–11; Ephesians 1:17–23; Matthew 28:16–20

It is a pervasive feature of biblical texts that God's way of saving us from our destructive ways is to work through human beings. Hence God chose the people of Israel and certain people within Israel. According to their own witness in the Old Testament, the people of Israel stumbled badly at times but kept their faith in the God who had chosen them and lived in hope that 'in that day' their God would bring his saving purpose to fulfillment.

For Christians this theme reaches its climax in Jesus who sets out to save us by forming a new community of human beings who will do God's will. This plan of salvation unfolds in three key stages. The first is the community of disciples, with its core group the twelve apostles. In continuity with the Old Testament, this foundational or first group is Israelite; the number twelve is a clear echo of the twelve tribes of Israel. As the gospel texts make clear, despite all Jesus' teachings, miracles, and warnings, this core group failed him dismally in its first great crisis—Jesus' passion, death and resurrection. Two betrayed him openly (Judas and Peter) while the rest fled.

But another characteristic teaching of the Bible comes to the fore at precisely this point. Instead of sacking this bunch of failures, as most leaders or institutions in our society would do, the resurrected Jesus pursues them and reestablishes them as his foundational community. As he meets them in Galilee they are still a broken, fragile group. Only eleven of them now, with Judas dead, and some of them still doubting. In an extraordinary gesture of confidence and trust, Jesus entrusts this unlikely crew with stage two of the divine plan—the establishment of a community of believers that embraces all nations. This fragile, fearful little group will paradoxically become the sign and instrument of God's universal purpose.

Their mission is not to set up a kingdom, a new nation, or a community in their own image and likeness. Rather, they are to baptise all nations 'in the name of the Father and of the Son and of the Holy Spirit'. This is the identifying characteristic of the new community, they do not belong to anyone else but God. The ascension supplies the perfect symbol of this universal mission and worldwide community. The ascended, heavenly Jesus is, in the words of the letter to the Ephesians, the one 'who fills the whole creation'; hence he can, as he promises in the gospel reading, 'be with you always; yes, even to the end of time'. A sign of Jesus' ongoing presence and a guarantee that the fledgling community will have the wherewithal to carry out its mission is the promise of the Holy Spirit ('you will receive power when the Holy Spirit comes on you and then you will be my witnesses . . . to the ends of the earth'). Jesus ascends to the Father (an assurance in faith that the resurrected one is with God) so that they may pour out the Spirit on disciples who will then be empowered to carry forward God's work.

Stage three in this divine plan is the glorious inheritance that the saints of all nations will receive from the God of Jesus Christ, the Father of glory, in the age to come. The pledge that all this will indeed happen is the manifestation of God's power in the life, teachings and works of Jesus, in particular his death and resurrection. Those eleven scattered and bewildered men, and the other disciples such as the women who followed Jesus, all testify to this manifestation and we are invited to believe their testimony.

The ascension, which stands between the resurrection and Pentecost, expresses in a very appropriate way the triumph of God's purpose that is the resurrection; it also points to our own exaltation that is achieved through our healing and empowerment by the Holy Spirit. All this has been done for our sake; all we need is to do our all for God's sake.

Pentecost Sunday

Acts 2:1–11; 1 Corinthians 12:3–7, 12–13; John 20:19–23

The first reading from the Acts of the Apostles has had, and continues to have, a powerful influence on our understanding of the feast of Pentecost. In particular, two images—which Luke presents as similes—tend to attract our attention, the mighty wind and the tongues of fire. But note how circumspect Luke's description is: he says 'they heard what sounded *like* a powerful wind', and saw something 'that seemed *like* tongues of fire'. It catches nicely the sense of something tangible, able to be experienced, but mysterious and ultimately indescribable. The reading from John's Gospel tells how Jesus breathed the Holy Spirit on the disciples. Two completely different presentations but both deriving from the same Hebrew word '*ruach*' which, depending on context, can mean wind, storm, breath, spirit. Thus, one can translate Genesis 1:2 as 'a wind from God', 'an almighty storm', 'a breath of God', 'the spirit of God'. Something of the transcendence and immanence of God is expressed by one tiny Hebrew word. In the story of Israel's deliverance from oppression in Egypt, '*ruach*' is the divine wind or storm that blows the sea back, while the pillar of fire provides Israel with light.

The scene in Acts evokes something of this transcendent divine power, but with an immanent touch. What seems like a roaring wind is the Holy Spirit that fills every part of the house, while what seems like tongues of fire settles on each one of them without singing a hair! The two similes emphasise that the Spirit reaches all and is for all—no favourites. All are infused with the Spirit and all receive the same gift—of speaking in different languages. Within the context of the Acts passage, this shows that it is the same Spirit in all. Moreover, as the reading from 1 Corinthians reminds us, this one Spirit or breath is a creator as in Genesis 1:2, not a destroyer or a cloner. Through the power of the Spirit each language is transformed so that it becomes more fully Parthian or Elamite or Greek as each proclaims the marvels of God. This also shows that there is no one sacred language in Christianity or, to put this another way, all languages are sacred.

Through the power of the Spirit, each individual is transformed and becomes more fully the particular individual he or she is meant to be. Similarly, each community becomes more fully that particular community. And what is even more amazing about the gift and power of the Spirit, as each individual and community becomes more perfectly itself, so the whole community of the church becomes more perfectly and fully itself. As Paul emphasises in the reading from 1 Corinthians 'there is a variety of gifts but always the same Spirit . . . working in all sorts of different ways in different people'.

In keeping with the Old Testament similes that it borrows, the passage from Acts focuses on the visible and the aural. The gospel passage deals with what is normally not seen or heard because it is within and is what we like to keep secret—our sin. Here the '*ruach*' is like the air we breathe: it enters into us and transforms our own spirit, our sinful self. In Matthew 9, Jesus asks some scribes which is easier, to say, 'your sins are forgiven,' or to say, 'stand up and walk'. Then, to show them that he has authority to forgive sins, he tells a paralyzed man to stand up and go home. You can tell someone that their sins are forgiven but there is no way of verifying it: there need be no external change. But, if you tell a paralysed person to get up and walk and nothing happens, then your reputation as a miracle worker is in deep trouble. Jesus heals the paralyzed man to encourage both him and the scribes to believe that he has the authority to bring about that inner, spiritual healing of which we are all in need. Once we accept this, our relationship with him, and his with us, can never be the same. If Jesus is able to touch our inmost being in this way then he must also know us better then we know ourselves—not to cause us anxiety but to bring us freedom from what causes anxiety. Our transcendent God becomes completely immanent in us to enable us to transcend our sinful selves. A striking feature of the gift of the Holy Spirit in John's account is that this transforming power is bequeathed to the community in an ordinary human way, by Jesus breathing and speaking.

Trinity Sunday

Exodus 34:4–6, 8–9; 2 Corinthians 13:11–13; John 3:16–18

The feast of the Trinity draws the three preceding feasts together. The Resurrection focuses on the Father as the life-giving one, the Ascension on Jesus as the vindicated and exalted one, Pentecost on the Holy Spirit as the empowering one. The readings for year A of this feast prompt us to reflect on how the Trinity comes to be revealed in the Bible and the challenge that this presents for us who believe it. Thus, the first reading takes us back to a foundational episode in the story of Israel—the apostasy of the golden calf. But this episode presupposes an even more foundational text of the Bible—Genesis 1:26 where humanity is made in the image and likeness of God. Given the iconoclastic stance of the Old Testament this does not refer to a visual likeness. More likely, as the remainder of the verse suggests, we are meant to be an image of God in our dominion over creation. That is, we are meant to emulate God's just and righteous rule of creation. It is not about how we look but about how we live. However, as the Bible goes on to teach us in the 'Garden Story', we tend to reverse things and make God in our image and likeness. The trouble is, the idea of God that we conjure up is a distorted one. In the 'Garden Story' the wily serpent tricks the woman into imagining a God who is mean and unjust. When we operate on a distorted image of God, we inevitably end up with a badly distorted image of ourselves (the couple have to hide from each other behind fig leaves, and to hide from God). Same couple, same God but now seen in a different and distorted light. The golden calf story takes this a step further by telling how Israel made what it regarded as an appropriate image of God and how chaos ensued. This happens as God is instructing Moses in the preceding chapters of Exodus to build a sanctuary so that God can live among the people.

Our first reading comes at the end of this story; a crucial step in Israel being reconciled to God is that it be reminded who God is and, just as importantly, how God acts. And so we have the proclamation of what one might call the divine 'code of conduct'—how God is gracious and merciful, slow to anger and abounding in steadfast love. Unfortunately, an important element of this 'code' is not included in the reading for the feast, namely that God will visit the iniquity of the parents on the children to the third and fourth generation. The Old Testament is here juxtaposing two primary images of the divinity that course through the Bible in a dynamic and at times tense relationship: God who is just and punishes evil and God who is merciful and forgiving. The Torah that has been given to Moses and that Israel has promptly disobeyed, is reinstated via two tablets of stone to replace the ones that Moses smashed. Obedience to the Torah will enable Israel to enjoy the presence of God in its midst and to act in an appropriate way when in the presence of God; namely as a just and merciful society.

However, as the prophets testify, the tendency to reverse the order of things runs long and deep. And so, as the Gospel of John testifies, God makes the extraordinary move of sending the perfect image of divinity, the Son, in our image and likeness: Jesus comes among us as one like us in all things but sin. By listening to him speak and act two revelatory moments take place. We are able, in faith, to 'see' the Father from whom he comes and whom he reveals. As well, we are able to see how we are, or rather can be, made in the image and likeness of God. In order to achieve this, two things are needed. We must first accept the judgment that we are in need of being remade because, if we judge ourselves we almost inevitably get it wrong. Along with this judgment, we must also accept the remedy—the gift of God's grace that transforms us and makes us Christ-like; remade in the image of the Son as the Son is the perfect image of the Father. The sign and guarantee of God's purpose, a purpose that will be fully realised, is the presence and power of the Spirit. It is through the power of the Spirit that a community is 'created' in the image and likeness of the perfect community, the Trinity. As Genesis signals at the beginning, we are not in the image and likeness of God as individuals so much as community ('male and female he created them').

Body and Blood of Christ (*Corpus Christi*)

---

*Deuteronomy 8:2–3, 14–16; 1 Corinthians 10:16–17;
John 6:51–58*

There is a famous Capuchin 'church of the bones' on the equally famous Via Veneto in Rome. As you emerge from walking through the gallery of neatly piled bones of the deceased—who desired to be buried for a time in a piece of the holy land that had been brought there—there is a message from the other side of the grave. I hope that I render the Italian reasonably accurately as 'what you are, we once were; what we are you one day will be'. While it may sound a bit macabre—or brutally honest and realistic—I could not help thinking that those clever Capuchins who composed this message meant it to be read on two levels (at least). The immediately obvious meaning is that it refers to our inevitable earthly demise, in the end we are added to the growing pile of bones. On the level of faith however, one is invited to look at the bones or through them to the eternal life that the 'speakers' now enjoy. Seen as such, their words are not a grim reminder but a promise. One can see a similar double entendre in the reading from Deuteronomy; 'he fed you with manna . . . to make you understand that man does not live on bread alone'. The abundance of manna as food is meant to point to the even greater abundance of spiritual gifts that God bestows on Israel ('everything that comes from the mouth of the Lord').

In the Eucharist, we believe that an unbreakable bond is established between us and our risen Lord who was once born like us, grew up and grew older as we do, and died as we all will do. He was like us in all things but sin. Now he is our risen and eternal Lord who comes to us in the Eucharist to feed us for the journey to the same 'home'. It is as if Jesus says to us 'what you are I once was, what I am now you one day will be'. Jesus did not offer his followers a program or blue print for transforming society.

He did not come to lead a revolution against the Roman occupation. He didn't even wipe out slavery although no doubt he had the power to do so. What Jesus did was offer himself completely to others in love as he offers himself to the Father and the Spirit. That is, he offered us a share in God's community, a life that would free all from the deathly evil that afflicts us. One can say that Jesus' presence to his earthly community was the very embodiment of love; his physical presence through words, gestures, embraces, sharing food and drink, time and space was a powerful sign of this commitment to others. But, as has been said, if you love like this you will be killed. Jesus' own death provides the occasion for the greatest gesture of love; the giving of his life for others. 'This is my body which is given for you; this is my blood which will be poured out for you.'

Jesus dies as all on earth are destined to die but his death and resurrection puts an end to the power of death. That which from a human point of view looks to be an unbridgeable chasm is bridged by the death and resurrection of Jesus, there is now continuity and communion between those of us on this side of death and those on the other side. Our risen heavenly Lord is present to us in the Eucharist and in this sacramental presence is more bodily present than he was during his earthly life. The resurrected body is after all the perfection of the human being. The way human beings are present to one another is through their bodies. The Old Testament catches this nicely by speaking of human beings as 'living flesh' with the breath of God in them. As the perfect human being, Jesus is now able to be bodily present in the sacrament to any people whenever the Eucharist is celebrated (it is not a physical presence).

But Jesus comes to us in the eucharistic presence, not simply to be with us on earth but also to bring about our own perfection. In the Eucharist we have the intersection of the present and the future. Jesus comes to us in order that we may be fed with his body and blood, the heavenly human food that transforms our mortal, dying, bodies into the likeness of his resurrected body. 'Anyone who does eat my flesh and drink my blood has eternal life, and I shall raise him up on the last day'. What he now is we will one day share in fully.

Second Sunday of the Year

Isaiah 49: 3, 5–6; 1 Corinthians 1:1–3; John 1:29–34

The first Sunday of the year celebrates the baptism of Jesus; this Sunday we move from the baptism to the mission of the one baptised—in John the Baptist's words Jesus is the lamb of God 'who takes away the sin of the world'. John then gives an account of his own 'mission'—it was to proclaim that someone greater than he was coming and that he would baptise with the Holy Spirit. Twice John says 'I did not know him myself'; it was only via the heavenly voice that he was able 'to see' and bear witness about Jesus. John's admission that he did not know Jesus until his presence and identity were revealed can be linked to his earlier statement to the Pharisees' delegation that 'Among you stands one whom you do not know'. Like John, they cannot know Jesus unless he is revealed to them; his identity is an integral part of his mission to take away the sin of the world. There is a distinct echo here of the Old Testament theology that all God does for Israel (God's 'mission') is in order that God's name may be known and confessed (identity). Once God is acknowledged as God the identity and purpose of everything else can be seen.

This bond between identity and mission in the figure of Jesus is powerfully expressed in the title that John the Baptist uses to describe him, 'the lamb of God'. Within a biblical context, this immediately links Jesus to the Passover lamb of the exodus and to its 'mission' or purpose, which was to be sacrificed for the sake of Israel's deliverance from oppression. It also links him to the servant passages in the book of Isaiah, the second of which is our first reading (the others are Isa 42:1–4; 50:4–9; 52:13—53:12). This servant will bring God's salvation to the ends of the earth, not by conquest or violence but by suffering violence and rejection (Isa 53:1–7). In this way the old barriers between Israel and other nations, between 'us' and 'them' will be removed.

The Bible often portrays sin as a barrier, something that causes a divided self, that divides us from our brothers and sisters and that divides us from God. The opening verses of Paul's First Letter to the Corinthians are a testimony from one who knows these barriers well but knows even better the healing power of the one who takes away the sin of the world. Paul, who saw himself as the worst of sinners, one who persecuted the church, is nevertheless able to refer to himself as one 'called to be an apostle' (a new mission that brings with it a new identity). Armed with this personal conviction, Paul is able to greet the Corinthians as those 'who are the holy people of Jesus Christ', and 'called to take their place among the saints'. The grace of Christ provides healing for each divided, sinful self. Equally, Paul conveys to the Corinthians his conviction that the grace of Christ has broken down the barrier between 'us' and 'them', between Jew and Gentile. Jesus 'is their Lord no less than ours'. God has no favourites; we are all called to be brothers and sisters in Christ. But our true identity and our fruitful relationship with our brothers and sisters rest of course on our foundational relationship with God: any barrier between ourselves and God will infect the other relationships. Paul highlights its importance by bringing his greeting to a climax with a prayer to 'God our Father'. Jesus' identity as 'Son of the Father' reveals the ultimate goal of his mission to take away the sin of the world—so that we can all share in their relationship as sons and daughters. This is the grace of God that alone brings us true peace.

Third Sunday of the Year

Isaiah 8:23—9:31; 1 Corinthians 1:10–13, 17;
Matthew 4:12–23 or 4:12–17

Jesus' first words in Matthew's Gospel as he commences his mission echo exactly those of John the Baptist in 3:2; 'repent for the kingdom of heaven is close at hand'. The use of the term 'heaven' is recognised as a Matthean substitution for the divine name: hence it is the equivalent of saying 'the kingdom of God'. There is continuity and development between the preaching of John and Jesus: Jesus is the one who incarnates the divine words proclaimed by John.

Matthew's account of the commencement of Jesus' mission is preceded by a report that he settled in Capernaum on the borders between Zebulun and Napthali and that this was in fulfillment of a passage from the book of Isaiah, our first reading. In its Isaian context, the passage proclaims a reversal of the humiliation that these two northern tribes, and other territories of the northern kingdom of Israel, suffered at the hands of the Assyrian invasion in the eighth century BCE. Those who were reduced to virtually nothing by the Assyrian advance will one day flourish again and rejoice.

The location of Capernaum on the border between the two territories allows Matthew to use the Isaian text as part of his 'portrayal' of the kingdom of heaven that Jesus inaugurates. Unlike earthly kingdoms which are based in the centres of power—for the northern kingdom this was the tribe of Ephraim and the capital of Samaria, for the southern kingdom it was the tribe of Judah and the capital of Jerusalem—the kingdom inaugurated by Jesus begins on the fringes, where no one expects it or bothers to look. Being on the borders it is almost like 'no–man's–land', identified with no earthly power base. Within the Jewish context, it is as about as far removed from Jerusalem as one could get; within a Roman context, it is even further from the centre of the empire's power—Rome. Yet, from this insignificant place shines 'a great light', the light of the world.

For John and Jesus, the appropriate way to prepare for the coming of the kingdom of heaven is to 'repent'. The Greek term rendered 'repent' challenges listeners to a 'change' or 'conversion'. In our earthly kingdoms we are too often caught up in the struggle to obtain control; control over our own lives, control over the lives of others. We all want to 'rule'. One can enter the kingdom of heaven only if one gives up all earthly claims to power and receives instead the 'grace' of Christ, the power that changes us from pseudo masters into real disciples.

In our earthly 'kingdoms', we are careful to select only the 'right ones' to advance the aims of the kingdom—whether it be our church, business, education, etc. As Matthew tells it, Jesus seems quite happy to engage the first couple of strangers that he comes across: Simon and Andrew. They are certainly not the type that one would normally find in the halls of royal courts. We tend to spend a lot of time reflecting on the mystery of God's foreknowledge and plan of salvation and this is good, but it can tie us up in knots. The scene by the sea looks to me similar to the story of the birth of Jesus in Luke. There were shepherds close by and God commissioned them to go and proclaim the Good News of Jesus' birth. Why not? God trusts them to be loyal messengers as much as God trusts a king or queen, trusts you and me.

God's trust of fragile, flawed human beings is a theme that runs right through the Bible. Jesus chooses disciples, teaches them and entrusts them with his mission but when the crunch comes at the time of his passion, they all desert him. Yet he does not sack them as we tend to do in our earthly kingdoms; instead they are welcomed back and entrusted with even greater responsibilities. Such is the kingdom of heaven.

One can see this same spirit of trust alive in Paul as he confronts divisive factions in the Corinthian community. Rather than condemn or dismiss those involved in the factions, Paul appeals to them all as brothers and sisters, as members of the kingdom of heaven, and sets out at length to show how the work of each one is part of a larger work that is the salvation that comes through Christ. As Jesus' disciples had to learn the way of discipleship at times painfully, so also the disciples in the church at Corinth. It is the challenge, and adventure, that greets each generation.

Fourth Sunday of the Year

*Zephaniah 2:3, 3:12–13; 1 Corinthians 1:26–31;
Matthew 5:1–12*

In Matthew's Gospel, Jesus begins his ministry by proclaiming, like John the Baptist, that the kingdom of heaven 'is close at hand' (3:2; 4:17). He gathers his first group of disciples and his fame as a preacher and healer spreads. Crowds gather, he goes up the mountain—an echo of Moses in Exodus—and begins to teach his disciples and the crowds about the kingdom of heaven. In relation to this, it is significant that in Jesus' discourse on the beatitudes the first and last of those formulated in the third person are followed by the statement 'theirs is the kingdom of heaven'. While each beatitude has an accompanying statement, the context established by 3:2 and 4:17 suggests that the statements about the kingdom form a frame around the list. The ones in between spell out particular aspects of life in the kingdom of heaven. The focus on the kingdom of heaven is supported by the statement accompanying the final beatitude that is formulated in the second person plural. 'You', all disciples of Jesus who suffer 'on my account', will receive a great reward in heaven.

There is considerable debate whether the beatitudes are to be understood as a kind of ethical guide for entry into the kingdom or a series of blessings pronounced over those who are already heirs to it because they are poor, meek, pure in heart, etc. A sign that they are heirs to the kingdom will be the radical transformation of their present condition. To adopt an either–or position may not do justice to the flexibility of the gospel texts. On balance however, Luke's version seems to be closer to the second understanding whereas I read Matthew's version within the context of Jesus' earlier call to repent; that is, to undergo a complete change or conversion. Those who are willing to be so transformed will enjoy the blessings of the kingdom as their reward. What will this be? The context of the beatitudes would suggest it is presumably the joy of seeing in full the reversal of which each beatitude speaks.

If this is a fair reading, how might we reasonably interpret the Matthean version as a guide for living today within the kingdom of heaven? Some suggestions. The poor in spirit are those who recognise their limitations and weakness, and need for God and neighbour; contrary to the prevailing ethos of aggressive individualism. Those who mourn recognise that every human being is a son or daughter of God and so cannot tolerate their mistreatment or destruction. The gentle are those who do not seek control over others to dominate them. Those who hunger and thirst for righteousness are willing to forego a secure, comfortable life in order to help those in need. In its biblical meaning, righteousness is primarily about right relationships, the fundamental one that enables all others is the one with God. The merciful are those who see the good in their neighbours despite their failures and weaknesses (they do not indulge in the 'blame game'). They are pure in heart because they, in their turn, let themselves be seen for who they are: there is no deceit or concealment. Peacemakers are those who are prepared to change so that the barriers that divide human beings can be crossed and communion restored. Those persecuted for 'righteousness' sake' do not take the easy way out, do not opt out when the crunch comes. One could say that all these virtuous paths are summed up in the final beatitude addressed to 'you' because discipleship of Jesus is what we believe human life is or should ultimately be about.

Discipleship does not mean participation in a particular programme, learning certain skills, achieving certain outcomes (although it excludes none of these). Jesus takes people as they are, assures them they can do extraordinary things in their seemingly ordinary lives and leaves them free to decide how to do so. The only thing required is that in living the beatitudes, which are about healing relationships, we model ourselves on the foundational relationship—Jesus' love of us and complete trust in us despite our flaws and failures.

Given that Matthew's version of the beatitudes is an integral part of Jesus' call to repent and live the Christian life of discipleship, the reading from Paul provides a timely caution. We need to be wary of measuring 'our progress' in the beatitudes—like measuring the stages in a career. Each of them (as Luke's different version implies) is greater and more challenging than any attempt on our part to live it (for example to be pure in heart). In fact, our attempts to live by the beatitudes, honest and well meaning though they be, will inevitably reveal our inability to do so, will reveal our weaknesses and limitations. If we are honest, we will come to see our need for God's grace for 'without me you can do nothing'. We need to be ministered to as much or more as those to whom we minister. By the same token, in recognizing and accepting our weakness and need, we receive the blessings promised in the beatitudes.

Fifth Sunday of the Year

Isaiah 58:7–10; 1 Corinthians 2:1–5; Matthew 5:13–16

Jesus' description of his listeners as salt and light are preceded by his proclamation of the beatitudes that commence the famous 'sermon on the mount'. The message presumably is that if you live the beatitudes then you 'are the salt of the earth', you 'are the light of the world'. As we know, when you put salt into something it permeates the whole thing and changes its flavour, transforming it from being, say, bland to delightful. Similarly when you switch on a light in a room it illuminates the whole room. So Jesus is saying that the person who lives the beatitudes will change or transform the whole earth. It is a massive claim, particularly when you link it with the beatitudes. Being poor in spirit, a mourner, being meek and merciful and a peacemaker do not seem at first glance to be the kind of things that bring about global change. Aren't those world programmes to eradicate poverty and disease much more effective? Is that not where you can taste the salt and see light shining? What is even more challenging and against the grain of modern global thinking, Jesus' claim refers to any individuals—'you'. So you and I can change the world. Indeed, by living the beatitudes, we *are* changing the world as salt transforms food, as light transforms darkness. Jesus is not just talking about the future.

When we read Jesus' sayings about salt and light in relation to the beatitudes that precede them, they challenge our expectations of how to go about transforming our world. Indeed his words provide a timely warning about a temptation that we can fall into these days. Because we are so aware of the 'global' factor now and the massive programmes that are put into place in an attempt to eradicate poverty and disease, we wonder about the impact of our seemingly impotent individual gestures. We may contribute money but that is our 'little bit' and then take no further part in such ventures until the next 'begging brochure' arrives. We may also feel that there is no point doing something, such as reducing my use of the car, until there is a sufficient number doing so, the 'critical mass' that will have an impact. But the gospel message is that something should be done because one believes it is right, not because it requires a 'critical mass' of participants to be effective. Even if only one individual does what is right, what is the blessed thing to do, Jesus assures him or her that this is being salt of the earth and light of the world. It is changing the world because one good act has taken place. We may not be able to monitor its impact and as trusting disciples of Jesus this should not be our concern or cause anxiety. But he assures us that people will see the good work 'and give glory to your Father in heaven'. Once people make God the centre of their lives, then things can find their proper place.

The reading from Paul expresses the same thing in a somewhat different way. A major anxiety that Paul had in preaching to and working among the Corinthians was that he would get in the way between them and their encounter with the crucified Christ. The gospel is not something that can be spread through clever marketing and its spread monitored like stocks and shares. It is about a relationship with Jesus that enables God's work to be fully realised.

The instruction from Isaiah outlines the kind of gestures that enshrine the spirit of the beatitudes and it is evident that the prophet is thinking of the immediate world around us. The passage mentions another important benefit that springs from acting in accord with the beatitudes. It is not only that we contribute to the transformation of 'the earth' but we ourselves are transformed. In the words of the prophet 'your wound will be quickly healed over'. Discipleship, in the manner outlined in the beatitudes, not only brings healing to others but healing to oneself. One way in which this will happen is that the person who is genuinely poor in spirit, meek and merciful will of course welcome this ministry on his or her behalf from others. If not then the genuineness of one's own ministry would be in question.

Sixth Sunday of the Year

Ecclesiasticus 15:15–20; 1 Corinthians 2:6–10;
Matthew 5:17–37

One can imagine that Jesus' teaching on the mount about the blessed life would have raised questions, and some hackles, among the Jewish authorities. How does this teaching relate to their commitment to the Torah, both the written Torah and the oral Torah that became enshrined in the Mishnah? Given that the gospels were written in the latter part of the first century, one could also imagine that Paul's preaching on the Law would have generated considerable debate and some hostility among Jewish Christians, who maintained their commitment to the Torah. Our readings for today outline some important principles about the relationship between Jesus' teaching and the Torah/Law. And, as I hope to show in the reflection, this is not simply an intra–Judaism debate or even worse, passé. It is a matter that is very much alive today.

Jesus' opening statement categorically denies that there is any conflict between his teaching on the beatitudes and the Torah/Law and the Prophets.[4] Anyone who keeps the commandments of the law and teaches them will be considered great in the kingdom of heaven. This is the same assurance given to those who keep the beatitudes. But it is important to realise that this denial is set between two other statements that he makes about the Law and the Prophets. The first is that he has come not to abolish but to fulfil or complete them. His teaching claims to show what the ultimate purpose of the law is and that we can for our part fulfil this ultimate purpose of the law—through God's grace. The second is the statement about

---

4. It may be worth mentioning that the Hebrew word torah conveys a variety of meanings depending on context. It can mean our word law, a collection of laws or a code, and the more general sense of teaching or instruction. When applied to the Pentateuch or five books of Moses as a whole it carries this meaning.

the need for true virtue or righteousness. I take it that the Greek word is rendering the Hebrew term for righteousness (*tsedakah*) that conveys the sense of a 'right relationship'. Our relationship, our commitment to God and neighbour needs to be one of complete self-giving not one that is measured against obedience to a law code. Hence the person who is righteous in Jesus' terms will keep and teach the 'least of the commandments' as an expression of their complete devotion to God and neighbour. And this is the purpose of the law. There is no sense in Jesus' teaching that the law is an imposition and in this he is echoing the theology of the author of Ecclesiasticus ('He has set fire and water before you; put out your hand to whichever you prefer'). If it was imposed then we would not be free under the law. It is something that one chooses and follows willingly because it helps one see its greater purpose, a blessed relationship with God and neighbour.

Jesus then takes up a selection from the Decalogue (ten commandments) to flesh out his teaching. In each case his point is to show that the aim of the law is to try and prevent the rupture of right relationships (notice how in the case of murder Jesus uses the term 'brother' for one's adversary) and to foster right relationships. This is seeking righteousness/virtue and maintaining righteousness. Jesus' concern to emphasise the true purpose of the law implies of course that the opposite is lurking among his listeners. It all depends on one's attitude and we flawed human beings can use the law to divide rather than to unite what has become divided. Or, to put this another way, we can use the law to gain advantage over the other, to win the case. As our society becomes more litigious the divisive and competitive use of the law seems to become more acute. There is the litigant and the defendant; the lawyers battle on their behalf in court, one gets the money and walks out one door while the other gets the bill or a sentence and walks out the other door. We say that the law has taken its course (or has been manipulated?) but the parties involved remain divided and often enemies for life. There is no reconciliation and one wonders whether the life of the society has been enhanced or demeaned. Paul speaks of having a wisdom 'to offer those who have reached maturity'. The mature ones will presumably welcome this wisdom and live by it. We have had Jesus' wise teaching on the law and righteousness for around 2000 years yet one wonders at times how deeply it has entered our hearts and minds? I am not just referring to the law courts here but to our attitudes towards one another in society and church. Does the booming litigation industry reflect our own attitudes in a way? If so, it can only be transformed by a change in our attitudes. Legislation of itself won't achieve it.

Seventh Sunday of the Year

Leviticus 19:1–2, 17–18; 1 Corinthians 3:16–23;
Matthew 5:38–48

In last Sunday's gospel reading, Jesus selects a number of law cases to show how his teaching is an integral part of his overall mission to complete or fulfil the Law and the Prophets. Wherever you have law cases you have the issue of punishment: one follows the other as night follow day. Hence, in this Sunday's reading, which follows immediately on last Sunday's in the gospel, Jesus challenges his listeners to rethink their understanding of punishment. This will in turn help in their rethinking of the law. Instead of speaking about punishment for crimes committed perhaps we should speak of the appropriate response to sin. The requirement of 'eye for eye and tooth for tooth' refers to Exodus 21:24 and was designed, in the judgment of critical scholars, to put a stop to the human tendency to exact revenge by going one better ('you break my fingers, I will break your arms'). It is a rather graphic way of stating the old adage 'let the punishment fit the crime'.

While this presumably put a stop to unrestrained violence it could leave the aggrieved parties as much at odds as before. Two guys with black eyes or their teeth knocked out may be an advance over revenge killings and an effective deterrent to other disputants but may also be in danger of exacerbating divisions within society rather than healing them. It could impede the purpose of law which is to enhance the good order and harmony of society.

Jesus' remedy is to apply the teaching on the beatitudes. A striking feature of this section of his teaching is that it applies equally whether one is the innocent party (the victim of the 'wicked man') or the guilty party in a conflict at law. Whichever side of the dock you stand on you are called to be committed to living the beatitudes. Even if you are the worst kind of criminal (and Jesus' teaching is applicable beyond the courtroom) you are able to become just as effective a herald of the gospel as an innocent party. Such is the reach and power of God's grace. Within our flawed system of law we may expel or banish criminals but God does not; the invitation or call is always there, even to the most hardened sinner, to become righteous and to seek the establishment of right relationships. Thankfully, one still reads of cases in which hardened criminals are not only able to express remorse for their crimes but devote themselves to a life of repentance as well.

Jesus' commitment to righteousness and the formation of right relationships is abundantly clear in the section that follows in which he commands us to love our enemies as God loves them. God hates sin but loves sinners. God is as committed to the salvation of the wicked as to the just and we need to remember that we ourselves are the wicked or were wicked at some stage in our lives and quite likely to become so again. God's salvation or love is of course never imposed. If it were it would not be love. People are free to reject it and so, as disciples of Jesus, we must respect the freedom of others to reject our offer of love and reconciliation however painful this may be (tellingly symbolised in that double slap in the face). This section of the gospel which, as noted above, 'returns' to the theme of the beatitudes, reveals just how radical and challenging it can be to live by them once one considers some particular cases or examples.

The reading from Leviticus contains a refrain that runs through much of what has come to be called the 'Holiness Code', the code of laws in chapters 17—26: 'you shall be holy, for I, the Lord your God, am holy'. In levitical thinking holiness is not just a moral quality as we tend to think. Rather it means someone or something is 'set apart' or belongs to the sacred realm and manifests the presence of God in a special way. Israel as the chosen people belongs to God and reveals the presence of God in our world in a special way. Paul takes up this notion and applies it to members of the Christian community. They are temples of God and so are a special presence of God to each other. To violently destroy a temple was, and still is, regarded as a sacrilege. Even more so, says Paul, if you destroy the living temple of the Lord in your brother or sister. If we apply this to the gospel reading, we can say that Jesus is urging his listeners to see others, even their enemies, as temples of God. Hence loving their enemies is another way, a very challenging way, of loving God.

Eighth Sunday of the Year

Isaiah 49:14–15; 1 Corinthians 4:1–5; Matthew 6:24–34

We have three powerful images of God as food for thought in our readings for this Sunday. We will take them in the order they appear. The prophecy from Isaiah portrays God as mother to reassure listeners and readers of God's unconditional commitment to Israel: and this on two counts. The first is that God's commitment does not weaken or fail. Occasionally even mothers abandon or forget their children but God doesn't. The second is that God's closeness to Israel is even more intense and intimate than that between a mother and the baby at her breast. If you want another Old Testament image of the intimately close relationship between God and Israel check out Jeremiah 13 where Israel is pictured like a person's loincloth. It was that close between you and me, so God says, but now God's loincloth has become soiled and useless. It is not the kind of metaphor we are likely to use in our politically correct context today but thankfully, Old Testament prophets were freer beings than we, and inspired as well.

The second is that of judge, in the reading from 1 Corinthians. We tend to have a somewhat fearful idea of a judge these days; he or she is likely to put you away for a spell in gaol. We may see them as upholders of the law but do we see them as deliverers? This is how the Old Testament saw the judge. In a society that had no universities or research academies where 'truth' is established with as much scientific rigour as possible, 'truth' in biblical terms meant more 'reliability'. A true person could be counted on to speak honestly. Hence the centrality of law and judgment in Old Testament theology, with the law court located at the main gate, the most public part of the town. The judge was not someone to be feared but to be relied on to distinguish truth from falsehood and to deliver the one wrongly accused. Human judges may of course fail but one can count on God, the just judge, never to fail.

Paul was heir to this tradition and so had a very positive attitude to the notion of God as judge. He looked forward to his judgment with confidence and joy. Why? Because nothing escapes the Lord's scrutiny, even the secret intentions of men's hearts. So the Lord knows all about Paul, his good and bad, and has already delivered a judgment on him. What is it? That Paul is one of the Lord's trusted servants, like his fellow Christians, and the Spirit is working through him to advance the cause of the gospel. So why should not Paul, or anyone who tries to live the gospels as best he or she can, look forward to the final judgment when the Lord comes.

The third image or metaphor of God is that of Master in the gospel passage. Let us put this into contemporary terms and call God the 'boss'. The first thing is that God does not impose. We human beings get to choose our boss but Jesus warns that there is no neutral territory; it is one or the other. You cannot sit on the fence. To be agnostic about it is still to make a decision and it will have an impact on your loyalties. Jesus then goes on to compare the boss he wants us to serve ('your heavenly Father') with the one that he says is the very worst you can choose—yourself (the devil is not mentioned here).

Once we decide that we are in charge or are going to be in charge then, according to Jesus' teaching, we sell ourselves short. We enslave ourselves (worry about our life) instead of freeing ourselves, and we confuse parts of ourselves with the real self (surely the body is more than clothing). All this worry and search for perfection on our terms ends up demeaning us; we settle for something much less than what we are and, as Jesus says, we are worth much more than the birds of the air that God cares for. If we choose our heavenly Father as the master or boss and become committed to the establishment of God's kingdom of righteousness on earth, then God will look after us. God is the most reliable and thoughtful boss. To put this another way, once we make God the centre of our lives, then God makes us the centre of divine life. We become temples of the Lord and our Lord is utterly devoted to building us into the most perfect of temples.

Ninth Sunday of the Year

Deuteronomy 11:18, 26–28; Romans 3:21–25, 28;
Matthew 7:21–27

Jesus says that the person who will enter the kingdom of heaven is the one 'who does the will of my Father in heaven'. The question is, what is the will of the Father and how do I know the will of the Father in my life? Jesus' statement comes towards the end of Matthew's sermon on the mount and one might well appeal to the contents of the sermon as spelling out the will of the Father. In a sense this is true but the sermon is a limited combination of some general instructions and specific laws. An example of a general one is 'let your light shine before others' in 5:16. An example of a specific one is 'whoever marries a divorced woman commits adultery' in 5:32. One has only to read through these chapters to see that they do not provide a complete blueprint for Christian life. When you think about it, there is no piece of legislation that could hope to cover the details of society's life, let alone the details of every member of a society. Those who have tried this kind of thing impose what we call totalitarian regimes and, thankfully, the long suffering citizens of such societies eventually get rid of them in the name of freedom.

Some think that the Old Testament is where legalism is to be found whereas we in the New Dispensation have been delivered from all that. But there are only 613 laws in the Old Testament and many fewer in the book of Deuteronomy from where our first reading comes. This is hardly a monument to legalistic control and indeed the Jews have a tradition of the oral torah that enables them to fill in the numerous gaps of the written Torah (a little like the distinction in Catholicism between Scripture and Tradition). Just by way of comparison, the latest Code of Canon Law has 1752 laws yet it provides canon lawyers with plenty of work adapting them to specific cases.

So, what is the will of God for us? From the way the gospels invite and challenge us to a faith commitment, I think God's will is that we make responsible decisions about our lives; in other words exercise our conscience. God frees us from the slavery of sin and bestows on us the dignity, the right to make decisions. This is a crucial component of being human. Of course, where there are rights, responsibilities follow closely. We have a responsibility to form our conscience so that we make responsible decisions. This is what biblical texts like the Torah and the Sermon on the Mount are designed to do, and the teaching of the church is designed to do. They provide us with crucial principles and guidelines but they do not take away the right that is ours as disciples to make decisions.

Hence Moses in Deuteronomy sets the alternatives before the people and leaves it to them to make the decision. They are called to obey the commandments he has set before them but note, to also follow 'the way I have marked out for you'. Moses sets them on their journey into the land but he cannot, and God will not, legislate for every step of that journey. The Torah provides them with the wherewithal to make decisions; God entrusts that dignity, freedom and responsibility to them. Anything less would impugn the theology of God that Deuteronomy is presenting.

In a similar way, Jesus distinguishes between listening to his words and acting on them. The person who makes decisions in accord with Jesus' teaching to the best of his or her ability is doing the will of God. Even though our decision making may, from a human point of view, look fragile at times and based on limited knowledge, it is the rock solid way to build a life because it is doing God's will. Moreover God is with us in this endeavour because, as Paul points out to his Roman audience, those who have faith in Jesus are justified by the free gift of God's grace. We do not have to pass an obedience test first in order to win God's love (we are not God's pets). We can only love God because God first loves us. Our obedience is a loving response to God's creative love.

Much of life is about making decisions and the great thing about our faith is that it gives us the confidence (through the assurance of God's grace) to make them. Even if we say that we will do whatever the pope or bishop or boss says, we have still made a decision. To say 'I won't make a decision on that' is still a decision. We cannot escape this fundamental aspect of life so why not get involved and make the best decisions we can? We will certainly make mistakes because we are human but this should encourage us to decide to do better next time, something that God surely applauds—it is doing God's will.

Tenth Sunday of the Year

Hosea 6:3–6; Romans 4:18–25; Matthew 9:9–13

If we take the initial lines of the reading from Hosea that quote the people, they look like a genuine expression of faith, hope and love; those three key virtues or values by which human beings live. There is the faith commitment to God ('Let us set ourselves to know the Lord'), there is the sure hope of God's gracious response ('that he will come is as certain as the dawn'); all this is a genuine expression of love, surely. Yet the following verses mock the people by contrasting their love (like a bit of morning fog, like dew which dries up at the first heat of day) with God's love (like showers and spring rain). The prophet knows that their hearts are wedded to Baal worship and their profession of loyalty to the God of Israel is a sham that must be exposed for what it is by the prophetic word.

We make professions of faith every week at our liturgies, some of us every day. Do our repeated failures to live up to them make a similar mockery and reduce them to empty words, like the people targeted in the first reading? How would we react if a prophet like Hosea came into our liturgy and condemned our confessions of faith, hope and love? How can we be sure that our faith, hope and love are genuine?

The second reading from the letter to the Romans and the Gospel reading from Matthew provide some help here. Paul's portrait of Abraham as the great father of faith is a stirring but highly condensed one, designed to fuel faith in his listeners. The book of Genesis, from which Paul no doubt drew his portrait (as well as Jewish tradition), is worth looking at briefly because it reveals a journey of faith that was not easy, and there were failures on the way. Twice Abraham passes his wife off as his sister when in foreign territory, relying on his cunning rather than God's promise (cf chapters 12; 20). He takes Hagar as a concubine when his wife Sarah is unable to have a child, even though the promise of an heir is to come through her (chapter 16). In chapter 15, he complains to God about his lack of an heir. In the end however, Abraham does come through as a true father of faith in the dangerous story of the binding of Isaac (chapter 22). What strikes me in reading the story of Abraham is that at no point, unlike the people in the book of Hosea, does he claim to be a man of faith. It is the angel who does this, who steps in to rescue Isaac and who says to Abraham 'now I know that you fear God'. Perhaps the message of this story is that we should be wary about claiming that our faith is secure and strong. Making such a claim may be a sign that it is weak. Let God and our neighbour be our judge; our role is to be as faithful as we can. They say that in India it is the people who discern that a holy man or woman is a guru; the person never makes the claim, to do so would be a sign that he or she is not a guru.

The message from the Gospel of Matthew is that true faith, hope and love are strongest in those who recognise how weak and inadequate their own faith hope and love are and who are glad and relieved to have this revealed to them and to all and sundry. I refer of course to Matthew the tax collector and his mates from the tax office who are made welcome at Jesus' table. From one point of view, to be made welcome at the master's table is a step up in society for these taxmen who were despised by both Romans and Jews. This certainly lies behind the comments made by the Pharisees. And indeed, associating with Jesus is a step up in society, but not in the way that the Pharisees—and perhaps even the taxmen—envisaged. Jesus identifies them as sinners and that he is the doctor who has come to heal them. Far from being put on the medical staff (the virtuous), the taxmen find themselves as patients in the casualty ward (the sinners). Yet they do not get up and walk away from Jesus and his company. They stay, even though they have been 'exposed' as sinners. Again, this is true faith, they trust that the one who is able to judge their most fundamental need is the one who can meet that need and who, as judge and healer, acts for no other motive than love. With faith like this, my weakness becomes my strength.

Eleventh Sunday of the Year

Exodus 19:2–6; Romans 5:6–11; Matthew 9:36—10:8

We all love peak or privileged experiences. We believe they have a profound impact on us and can radically change the way we live. But there are two issues that we need to take into account when we reflect on peak experiences—especially when they concern our relationship with God. The first is what constitutes a peak or privileged experience of God? The second is how do we know that it has really, radically changed us?

The reading from Exodus provides some food for thought. The people have experienced liberation from slavery in Egypt and now they are invited into an intimate and privileged covenant with the God who delivered them, who speaks to them from the mountain via Moses the chosen mediator. They are, as a nation, to be consecrated as God's priestly ministers to the rest of the world. The mountain, the cloud, the thunder and lightning, the voice, all signal a powerful experience of the presence of the divinity. Israel readily agrees to the terms of the covenant and the deal is sealed at the foot of the mountain in Exodus 24. But then Moses is summoned up the mountain and things go quiet. Same God, just as present on the mountain as before (the cloud is still there), but now for those below there is silence and waiting. The people judge that this is an absence of God not a presence and set out to make gods whose 'presence' they can control (carry around as a statue). This text invites us to reflect that God is as present in the silence and waiting (the seeming 'absence') as in the intensity of the theophany on the mountain. It also invites us to reflect that what the Israelites see as a privileged experience of God does not change them at all. They remain as fickle as they were when confronted by the Egyptian forces at the Sea.

The gospel reading invites reflection on our perceived experiences of God by focusing on the exercise of divine power. As in the exodus story, Jesus has invited the twelve into an intimate relationship and now sends them out on a mission with power over unclean spirits and diseases. We all thrill to the exercise of power; to exercise the kind of power the disciples enjoyed must have been heady stuff indeed. One would think that this experience would secure their undying commitment to Jesus. But what happens? At the first major crisis (the contrary experience of Jesus as a powerless prisoner of the authorities) they abandon him to a man. Yet, as Paul takes pains to point out to his Roman readers, the experience of the suffering, reviled and crucified Jesus was as much a presence of the God of infinite power as the disciples' experience of casting out demons and curing the sick. Why so? Because it brought about our reconciliation with God, from whom we were estranged because of our sins. The passion of Christ completely rewrites our understanding of power and how it is exercised. In our modern world we find it difficult to equate power with the biblical notion of love as loyalty, particularly to the helpless and powerless. If we think of love in relation to power, it tends to be romantic love and sex. Our understanding of both words is warped. Only God can show us, through the experience of Jesus and his disciples that the ultimate power, divine power, is love and it is a transforming power.

I remember once being at a lecture given by the great Pauline scholar Ernst Käsemann, at which he said, 'thank God for the canon (of the Bible), otherwise we would all have our own canons'. We all have our favourite passages of Scripture and the danger is that we will neglect other passages, less attractive in our judgment, or more difficult or even off–putting. Something similar can be said about the experience of God. As devoted believers, we all hunger for the experience of God and rightly so. God entrusts to us the freedom and responsibility of judging whether this or that experience is of God. We all have our ideas of what an experience of God should be like and no doubt we draw on the Bible to forge these ideas. But there is the danger that we will have our favourite ideas, as we have our favourite biblical passages, and that we will forget those other ones that the Bible holds up for our consideration, above all of course that of the suffering and crucified Christ.

Twelfth Sunday of the Year

Jeremiah 20:10–13; Romans 5:12–15; Matthew 10:26–33

The famous passage from the letter to the Romans lends weight to the old saying that 'the more things change the more they seem the same'. Paul, like his contemporaries in the Jewish world, thought of Adam and Eve as a historical couple, just as they thought the sun circled the earth and that humans and animals had lived together from the beginning of creation. The impact of science and critical analysis of ancient texts means that we no longer think that way. The danger is that we may think we are smarter than folk of ancient times, that their myths (for example, the 'Garden Story') are *passé*. The achievements in science may mean that people one day will fly to a distant planet at warp speed. They may be incredibly well educated by our standards but they will face the same challenges that stone-age people, that Paul and his contemporaries faced—how to relate to their fellow men and women.

For all our technological achievements, are we any better at living the three great values or virtues that inform all human life—faith (in whom do I trust), hope (to whom do I look for motivation), love (to whom will I be completely loyal)? Paul no doubt saw Adam as a historical figure but he also saw the symbolic or representative significance of Adam in relation to humanity as such. In this he shared something with the modern understanding of the Garden Story in which Adam and Eve represent human beings as such. The contrast that Paul draws between Adam and Jesus proclaims his conviction that only the Christ can heal our inability to forge relationships with God and neighbour that are faithful, hope-filled and loving.

The Gospel passage from Matthew presents the same challenge—and the same hope—in somewhat different terms. The context is Jesus' singling out of the twelve and instructing them about their mission as his disciples. Matthew 10:1–42 is principally a teaching or torah about mission and discipleship, there is no report of the twelve going out on the mission. The initial instructions about how to conduct the mission (verses 1–15) are followed by warnings about the rejection and persecution that is likely (inevitably?) to accompany the mission (verses 16–33). The final section in verses 34–42 places this teaching within the larger context of Jesus' overall purpose/mission. Our particular passage (10:26–33) revolves around three occurrences of the command 'do not fear'. The first command in verse 26 can be related to faith: in the face of persecution, we must trust Jesus our master, work within this relationship and speak the gospel message as he has instructed us (boldly, in the words of Paul 'in season and out of season'). If we do not maintain faith in Jesus in times of trouble, then it is likely we will cut and run (which means that fear has won) or we will try and take charge on our own terms (which means that we are no longer preaching or living the gospel).

The second command in verse 28 can be related to hope. The persecutions, the violence that we see around us can drain our hope that the kingdom of God can ever be established on earth. Fear can drive me to try and shut out the world and the challenge of preaching the kingdom in the forlorn hope that I can secure the little world of my life. Jesus counters this by warning his disciples that such an attitude will not protect them from the 'one who can destroy both body and soul in hell' (I prefer this reading to the alternative, that it is a reference to God's final judgment). They should 'fear' this 'enemy'; or be on their guard, because to retreat like this is just what he wants them to do. In battle, an army is always at its most vulnerable when beating a retreat.

The third command not to fear in verse 31 can be related to love or, in more biblical terms, loyalty. Jesus assures the disciples that they are precious in his eyes and that he is their ever loyal advocate with the Father. In terms of the disciples' mission, Jesus will not only be their loyal advocate but—and he cannot be anything else—a true advocate. Hence, if they disown him (through fear), this will be brought before the Father. It does not mean that Jesus ceases loving those who disown him; an integral part of his loyal love is that we must know, and hopefully accept, that we have been disloyal.

One further feature of the mission of the twelve worth noting is that, although they are given power to heal and drive out evil spirits, they are not given power over those who persecute them. Presumably, this is because such power would involve violence and the power that Jesus exercises is not violent, as his passion and death clearly demonstrate. Jesus' Old Testament precursor here is Jeremiah, imprisoned in the stocks with only his faith and the conviction of his preaching to sustain him. And so he sings a little psalm. Yes this powerless, imprisoned prophet who preached for twenty-three years against the establishment to no avail (25:1) is the one whose message was in time accepted and treasured as God's life-giving word.

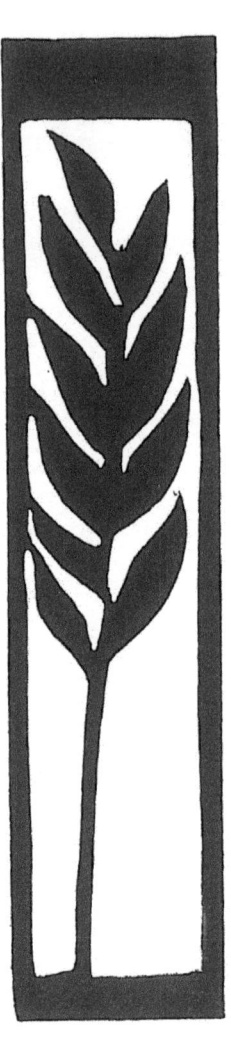

Thirteenth Sunday of the Year

2 Kings 4:8–11, 14–16; Romans 6:3–4, 8–11;
Matthew 10:37–42

Jesus says in the gospel passage that 'Anyone who welcomes a prophet because he is a prophet will have a prophet's reward'. The same goes for a holy man. The question is, what reward does a prophet or holy man bring and is not Jesus the prophet and holy man par excellence? Well, if we follow the lead of today's gospel it is certainly not the kind of reward that many would have in mind. You welcome Jesus home to your family and he immediately takes centre stage. At least he does not impose himself but invites or challenges; he calls for a decision one way or the other (note the repeated 'prefer'). Still a mighty shock to the system and one which Christians of every generation struggle to come to terms with. And it is not just something that affects relationships within a family; Jesus claims that it involves one's whole life. If you give it up for his sake he promises you that you will find it.

This statement does provide a clue as to how to read his challenge about the family. One cannot add relationship with Jesus onto one's life as a kind of accessory, the icing on the cake. It must be the foundation of all other relationships otherwise it will not work, nor will they. Only when one has made Jesus the centre of one's life can all our other relationships find their true meaning and purpose: family, friends, the good the bad, etc. It amounts to a radical rethink of customary priorities. For example, to refuse to make Jesus the centre of one's life is to be disloyal to one's parents, family and friends, to sell them short. After all, the best thing for you is the best thing for them. This is a massive challenge for any human being but a merciful God has provided a simple way for us to get under way, and one that provides abundant grace to complete our transformation.

According to our reading from Paul, by undergoing the simple rite of baptism we join Christ in his death, which was a death for our sakes, in order that 'we might live to a new life'. So through baptism we are welcomed into the family of Jesus, a family that lasts forever.

What is our reward then? I think it is this, that when we welcome Jesus as the honoured guest, the centre of our life, he becomes our host who then treats us as honoured guests, and even more than guests, as beloved sons and daughters of his father. But how do we know that we are really welcoming Jesus into our lives, into our families? The last part of the gospel provides an answer. When we welcome someone not because of what he or she can do for us but simply because he or she is a disciple and thereby an honoured guest, no matter how 'little', then we have welcomed Jesus into our lives. This is so because anyone who welcomes a disciple in this way 'welcomes me'.

The reading from 2 Kings introduces a powerful story that touches on this same theme. Let a prophet into your life and it will never be the same again. But there is a nice twist to the end of this story. Not only is the life of the 'great lady of Shunem' turned upside down as a result of providing hospitality to Elisha, but Elisha's status as a prophet is turned upside down too. She gives birth to a son as Elisha foretells but he soon dies and the distraught mother hastens to the prophet and falls at his feet. Elisha dispatches his servant with his staff to raise the child but it does not work. Elisha has botched the job: one cannot presume to have the prophetic charism, it is a gift and God gives it to whomever God chooses and whenever God chooses. In this case, the woman is 'revealed' as the prophet, the one who knows the score. Elisha is obliged to 'follow her' and return to her house that he has turned upside down in order to resuscitate her son. It is a measure of Israel's realistic attitude to its tradition that it could tell a critical story about one of the great figures of the tradition.

Fourteenth Sunday of the Year

Zechariah 9:9–10; Romans 8:9, 11–13; Matthew 11:25–30

If we can, we like to be in control of things and even other people. It has become almost an obsession in our modern highly individualistic societies where I must plan my life and have it all unfold according to plan, even if this may involve trumping the plans of others. But, this is just healthy competition, is it not? Rich nations spend enormous amounts of money and effort bending nature to their will and bending other human beings to their will. A theme that runs through the Bible is that the more we try to take control of our lives, to have things on our terms, the more entrapped we become. One can see it in the Garden Story. Adam and Eve are promised by the serpent that they will be like God, supremely powerful and free, yet they end up hiding from each other and from God, powerless and afraid. We can see this kind of theme in each of this Sunday's readings.

In our first reading, the prophet Zechariah sees the arrival of a king who will free the warring kingdoms of Ephraim (the north) and Jerusalem (the south) from the trap of war into which they and other nations have fallen. Neither Ephraim nor Jerusalem can do this; they are completely trapped by the weapons they have made and the wars they have waged—all in the name of gaining freedom from the 'oppression' of the other, of gaining control on their terms. Only someone completely free of this trap, the humble peace-bearing king, riding a donkey, not in a chariot or on a warhorse, can free them. He will not return violence with violence. If they do not cede 'control' to this king, they will remain trapped.

The reading from Paul's letter to the Romans is about our futile attempts to control our personal lives and to have things on our terms. Paul knows that we will go to any lengths to try and banish the fear of death from our lives; it is after all the ultimate sign that we do not have control of life and that eventually it comes to and end no matter how hard we fight against it. Our desperate attempts to thwart death lead, according to Paul, to unspiritual lives. Living such lives 'you are doomed to die'. Paul is not just talking about physical death here but the death of our spiritual self that is the fruit of unspiritual lives. The antidote is to welcome the Spirit of God who has made a home in us and to recognise that it is the presence of this Spirit in us that alone can enable us to escape the clutches of both physical and spiritual death. Paul's conviction that the Spirit has made its home in us reminds me of Jesus visiting the home of Martha and Mary. Like Mary, we should sit and listen to the teaching of the Spirit about how to live our lives, rather than try and control things on our terms like Martha.

The gospel passage tackles our obsession with being in control in three moves. The first identifies the ones who can freely and openly receive Jesus' teaching. They are not the learned and clever who think they are in control but those who like children, accept that they need to learn from 'the other'. The second identifies Jesus as the sole source of the teaching; the knowledge of the Father that alone can save. To whom does Jesus choose to reveal the Father? The answer comes in the third move where Jesus invites 'all you who labour and are overburdened'.

Within the context of the interpretation that I am presenting here, the overburdened are not so much those who are crushed by others (although these are not excluded) but those of us who try to take control of our lives on our terms and who therefore have to keep acquiring more and consuming more (the more you have the greater the appetite). In fact we become trapped and in order to be free of this yoke we need to take on the yoke of Jesus. Doing this of course means becoming a disciple. Taking his yoke does not mean that he unloads his burden onto us, rather we form a team with him. The image that comes to mind is of a team of oxen yoked together and ploughing the land. One can come across some very unusual teams in the Middle East among poor farmers; a donkey and ox, a donkey and horse, occasionally even a farmer helping his ox along. This was probably the case also in Jesus' day. Paradoxically, by taking on the yoke of Jesus, what looks to be the oddest team of all—myself the sinner and the Son of God—becomes the perfect team. What looks impossible becomes easy to bear (because Jesus is with us sharing the yoke) and gives rest and refreshment rather than exhaustion. The yoke of the cross that was imposed on Christ by his apparent victors—the forces of evil—becomes the sign and instrument of his victory over these forces and salvation for all the overburdened and oppressed.

Fifteenth Sunday of the Year

Isaiah 55:10–11; Romans 8:18–23; Matthew 13:1–23 or 13:1–9

We have two views about the word of God in this Sunday's readings; one that emphasises the transcendence and power of God's word, the other that emphasises its immanence, its presence in human beings. The reading from Isaiah proclaims that the word that issues from God's mouth always achieves what God wills it to achieve; its purpose cannot be thwarted. And what is its purpose? The text employs the simile of life giving rain and snow to assert that God's purpose, as revealed via his word, is to give life and nourishment. Given the setting of the so-called 'Second Isaiah' (chapters 40—55) with the people languishing in Babylonian exile, confronted by the claims that the Babylonians no doubt made about the power of their gods over all other gods, this is a bold assertion. One catches glimpses in chapters 40—55 of a prophet striving to overcome doubt and despair among his audience—see 40:27–31 for an example. But this claim about the power of God's word is an integral part of Israel's faith; even God's word of judgment against sinners has this same purpose in mind: once a sinner accepts the word of judgment, life-giving forgiveness follows.

The famous parable of the sower in Matthew's Gospel explores the other side of the equation: the immanence of God's word. If we read the parable without the subsequent explanation God looks like a reckless farmer, casting seed on good as well as bad terrain. What a waste from someone who presumably knows the difference better than anyone else! But God will try anything to get a harvest and, as with the Isaiah text, the parable finishes on a confident note: despite what looks to be a terrible waste of good seed on poor soil, there will indeed be a rich harvest. God's word will ultimately be fruitful. One could almost read the parable as an allegory of the mission of Jesus.

If we take the subsequent explanation of the parable into account, a somewhat different interpretation emerges. The word of God starts to look more fragile and vulnerable. It can be snatched away by the evil one, it can fail to transform the one who hears it so that he or she succumbs to the first trial or persecution. Is this the all powerful word of God? On reflection however, the interpretation or allegorising of the parable seems to make a subtle shift from the word of God as sown (by God, by Jesus, by a preacher) to the word of God as it enters the receiver, as 'it is sown in his heart'. In doing so it becomes one with the person, which is in keeping with the theology of incarnation. It does so to such an extent that the text can speak as one of the word and the person who hears the word.

This is evident where the text says 'what was sown on rocky ground (sic the seed/word), this is the one who hears the word of God and immediately receives it with joy' (following the NRSV which is closer to the Greek here than the Jerusalem Bible which is used in the Lectionary). The message is that as the word of God is sown in our hearts it becomes or is meant to become our word, an integral part of our life as disciples, an integral part of our discourse as disciples. Hence it enters fully into the fragile, vulnerable world of human beings and as such it can be abused and misrepresented, neglected or treasured. Thus it mirrors Jesus himself who became one like us in all things but sin and experienced abuse and misrepresentation, neglect and rejection (another angle on the notion of God as reckless, going to any lengths, withholding nothing). But, even though the word of God becomes one with us it does not cease to be the pure word of God (a parallel perhaps with the statement that Jesus was like us in all things 'but sin'). Awareness of this is surely an urge to treasure this word as a great gift, to protect it from abuse and to live it in a way that will reveal to others the source of our life.

An intriguing and somewhat difficult element of this Sunday's gospel is the section between the parable and the explanation, in which the disciples ask Jesus why he speaks in parables. As part of his answer he quotes Isaiah 6:9–10, itself a difficult passage that is rendered in a number of ways in the New Testament (and the Greek Septuagint). Two brief comments may be made here. The first is that this parable commences a series of seven parables on the kingdom (a perfect biblical number) and this signals an important stage in the unfolding of Matthew's Gospel. As well as this, the series comes after a number of encounters with Jewish authorities who are hostile to Jesus and his message. This hostility helps explain the exchange between Jesus and the disciples about the purpose of parables, as well as the emphasis in the explanation of the parable on those who reject the word. As the gospel presents it, the prophecy of Isaiah about the rejection of the word is being fulfilled even as Jesus speaks but, in the divine scheme of things, this is a foreseen prelude to the ultimate triumph over evil of Jesus and his word.

Sixteenth Sunday of the Year

Wisdom 12:13, 16–19; Romans 8:26–27;
Matthew 13:24–43 or 13:24–30

This Sunday's reading from Matthew contains parables two, three and four of the series of seven that begins with the parable of the sower (see previous Sunday). What binds these three parables together is the theme of the kingdom of heaven (this is widely thought to be Matthew's pious way of referring to the presence of God). Whenever I read this series of three parables I cannot help imagining a scene in which Jesus tells a story—which is what a parable basically is. The actual telling of the parable may have been much longer than the textual version we have: this could well be an outline, designed to provide sufficient information for preachers to develop into a homily or instruction. One could imagine that as Jesus the master preacher tells his parable questions arise among his listeners which lead to the second parable, which raises a further question or questions which in turn lead to the third parable—and three is a favourite number in biblical story telling. One gains the impression that each parable is designed to stimulate people to think, ask questions and make decisions. It is significant that a number of parables end with Jesus saying 'listen, anyone who has ears to hear': in our jargon, 'think about it folks'. In keeping with the Bible as an invitation to think rather than the imposition of thought, parables are meant to encourage people to reflect and make decisions about their lives. The Bible does not portray Jesus as imposing his teaching or will; to do so would impugn the biblical theology of God.

The first parable about the wheat and the darnel addresses the troubling question why evil seems to permeate and threaten the lives of good, faithful people who believe in a God of justice who is by definition intolerant of evil. If one's theology did not present God as intolerant of evil then who would be interested in following such a God? According to this parable, God (the sower) is portrayed as well aware of the conflict between good and evil and knows the best way of dealing with it. The wheat will be protected so that it can flourish; the darnel will not be allowed to overcome and destroy it. Thus, the situation is not out of (God's) control and good will ultimately triumph over evil at the harvest.

But parables, even those of Jesus, are limited human stories and cannot cover everything. The parable of the wheat and darnel could give the impression that good and evil are sort of evenly matched, at least until the harvest. How can you be sure you are on the winning side (the kingdom)? The second parable of the mustard seed, in my view, responds to this question or limitation in the preceding parable. It assures its listeners that the kingdom of heaven is the reality that grows vigorously and vibrantly; even though it may begin like a mustard seed in a tiny way it far outstrips any rival and becomes a tree that offers protection for all those who seek it (the birds).

Although the second parable answers a question that is likely to arise from the first one, it in turn raises another question—Jesus, you say that the kingdom of heaven grows from tiny beginnings like a mustard seed to become a highly visible and welcoming 'tree', but I don't see it growing in any visible way in my life. How do I know the kingdom is here? In answer, Jesus tells the parable of the woman mixing yeast in flour. Once mixed in with the flour, the yeast effectively disappears. All one sees is flour. But the yeast works its way invisible to the human eye and transforms the dough into something new and highly desirable. Even though the presence of God may appear at times invisible to human perception, it permeates all creation and is bringing about its transformation.

Parables are an ingenious way of preaching the word of God and Jesus was a master storyteller. But words are not the only way human beings communicate; indeed at times words, even the words that Jesus spoke, are not the appropriate way to respond to a situation—something that he of course knew very well. Paul assures his readers that when words fail us or are not the appropriate way to 'speak' to God, the Spirit enables us to express ourselves and our needs in the most appropriate way, a way that is 'according to the mind of God'. God listens as attentively to those who are lost for words as to those who are gifted with words. No one is left unheard. Well aware of this, the author of the book of Wisdom celebrates our God who 'cares for everything' in a way that is perfectly just and merciful.

Seventeenth Sunday of the Year

*1 Kings 3:5, 7–12; Romans 8:28–30;
Matthew 13:44–52 or 13:44–46*

We can apply the same kind of interpretation to this Sunday's group of three parables as to last Sunday's three. The two groups of three are separated by Jesus' explanation to the disciples of the parable of the wheat and the darnel. As noted earlier, the parable of the sower makes up a series of seven parables overall in this section of the gospel.

The previous group of parables emphasises the presence and initiative of God that is the foundational principle of the kingdom of heaven. Once this principle has been taught, the group of parables in this Sunday's reading can explore the various ways in which we human beings encounter the kingdom. The first one envisages someone stumbling on the kingdom 'by chance' like someone stumbling on treasure in a field. We can be cruising through life quite comfortably and something happens, we meet someone or have an experience and our lives are changed forever. On reflection, we discern the presence of God in the encounter. We have stumbled on the kingdom 'by chance'? But, given the previous group of three parables, the gospel is perhaps inviting us to think about whether our encounter with the kingdom can ever be just by chance. We might think so initially but, as they say, God works in strange ways.

Of course the apparent chance encounter with the kingdom may not be many peoples' experience. What of the person who searches and longs for an encounter with God, some reassuring experience of the divine, and never has it? The second parable about the merchant searching for fine pearls is designed to assure the seekers that 'seek and you will find, knock and the door will be opened to you'. The kingdom is worth struggling and searching for because it is like precious pearls. Once again, we might add that God always finds or meets the genuine searcher: he or she will not be left stranded or empty handed.

Both of these parables speak of the kingdom as something marvelous and wonderful. When you come across it you are so struck with delight and wonder that it absorbs your whole life. You will give up everything else to have it. But what of those who find that living the kingdom of heaven can often be ambiguous and confusing, full of difficult decisions? The third parable can be seen to respond to them by portraying the painstaking work of fishermen who must sift carefully through their catch and separate what they judge to be good fish from those that are of no use. But their painstaking work is rewarded and they take home a catch of fish. The value of this seemingly ordinary and even arduous living of the kingdom is emphasised by the way Jesus says that it mirrors the work of the angels at the end of time. They will take great care to ensure that the good are singled out and only the wicked thrown away. The theme of the end time links this parable to the earlier one about the wheat and darnel, and in this way a kind of frame is formed around the six parables on the kingdom of heaven (note that the parable of the sower does not itself refer to the kingdom).

As noted in an earlier reflection, parables are an ingenious way of teaching but, like all literary forms, they are limited. No one knew this better than Jesus. In the final section of our gospel he passes the mantle of speaking parables to the disciples. Once they have been schooled in his method of teaching, they are 'like a householder who brings out from his storeroom things both new and old'. That is, they will pass on the parables proclaimed by Jesus but also compose new ones and even new forms of teaching to meet new situations. This is an important aspect of being a disciple of Jesus, of loyally carrying on his work. In terms of Paul's letter, it is according to the purpose of God and God will co-operate with those who love him and turn their work to a good purpose. God will give us the grace to proclaim the gospel in ways both new and old. The old here is not something out-of-date; rather the way Jesus taught and the things that he taught become the foundation on which disciples of subsequent generations build.

One can be graced as a wise preacher and teacher but one can also lose or abuse the gift, just as one can lose the treasure of the kingdom or fail to follow up on a peak experience of God. The first reading from 1 Kings provides a reminder of this with Solomon. According to the text, he prayed at Gibeon and was given the gift of a 'heart wise and shrewd as none before you'. For a while Solomon used the gift well but he later abused the gift; the outcome was the schism in the united kingdom of David, a rift that was never healed and ended up contributing to the collapse of monarchy altogether.

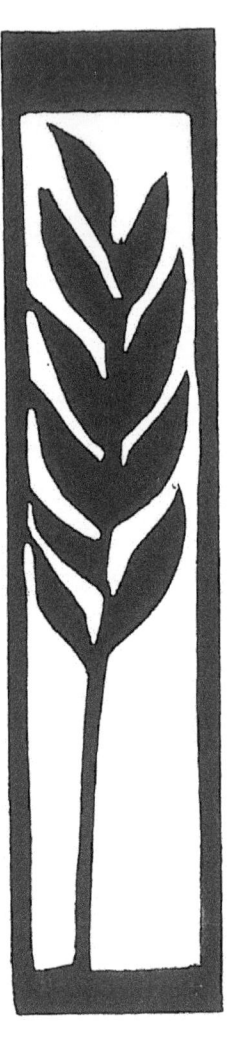

Eighteenth Sunday of the Year

Isaiah 55:1–3; Romans 8:35, 37–39; Matthew 14:13–21

Both Matthew and Mark's Gospels have two accounts of the miracle of the loaves and fish. In the first account of each, there are five loaves, in the second seven. What is fascinating about the accounts in both Gospels is that there is no recorded comment from the people about where all the food comes from. Rather different to the stories of Jesus healing sick people and casting out demons: often these are followed by a comment from the onlookers about who Jesus is and where he comes from. Why the difference? Is it because the feeding stories deal with the ordinary and everyday realities—having a meal, working one's job, buying clothes, cleaning the house, etc. They are not the sort of things that make one stop and think. Are we more likely to do so and turn to God when things are tough, as Paul urges his Roman readers to do, assuring them of the utter reliability of God's love?

Perhaps those who enjoyed Jesus' bountiful bread and fish are a bit like that modern, western phenomenon—the consumer. We have become so accustomed to our consumer world that, at least until scientists recently started ringing alarm bells, we took it all for granted. How many times have I asked myself when I fill the car with petrol, where does this fuel come from and how many people in say, the Middle East, may have been disadvantaged or even killed during its production? As I recall, hardly ever. And until recently, did I ever give a thought to what comes out the car's exhaust? All I am interested in is the availability of the product for which I pay and which I consume.

If my mind is so focused on the particular thing at this particular moment that I am consuming it then it is unlikely I will lift my head to see where it all came from and where it is all heading. It is even more unlikely that I will see with the eye of faith that a miracle has taken place, that in the flow of human life God has privileged me with a moment of grace. But God is kind and merciful and the Bible contains a number of stories in which God gently (occasionally more firmly) lifts our heads out of the consumer trough and invites us to see what is really going on and how extraordinary the ordinary can be when seen from the right perspective.

A rather nice example is provided by our reading from Isaiah. The text invites all and sundry to a marvelous banquet, one that boasts the best corn, wine and milk, not the shonky stuff that you buy in a market. And it is all free! The prospect of getting something for nothing always arouses human interest and at this point the text makes its real play. It invites those salivating over the prospect of a marvelous free feed to realise that such generosity can only come from God (listen to me and you will have good things to eat). What is more, the banquet of food is a prelude to the real gift that God is offering and that is an everlasting covenant. In a poetic yet subtle way, this prophecy urges its readers to realise that God is the source of any bounty that they enjoy and that it in turn is a pledge of the intimate relationship that God wishes to establish with them. In short, a moment of God's grace should enable them to see more clearly the whole purpose of God in their lives.

Similarly with the gospel. Even though Jesus knows the real plight and need of the crowd he seems happy enough to let them enjoy the moment of their miraculous meal. But it is a different matter with the disciples. His words and gestures clearly reveal this meal as something that takes what appears from a human point of view to be inadequate and turns it into an anticipation of the messianic banquet in the kingdom of heaven. What they cannot do (we have only five loaves and a few fish), Jesus enables them to do with abundance once they follow his instructions (twelve baskets of leftovers carefully collected). The parallel to be drawn is that if they wish to enjoy the kingdom of heaven as pictured in his parables, they should listen to him and do what he says as loyal disciples. But, as so often, they struggle to see beyond the moment and it is only in the light of Jesus' death and resurrection and the gift of the Spirit that they are able to revisit these events in his ministry and see their purpose and meaning. If this is the case with the disciples then I would suggest it is even more so in our age where the mood seems to be that the consumer is or should be the model of human life. We may find it even harder than the disciples to recognise the presence of God in our lives. The incarnational aspect of Christianity, being able to immerse oneself fully in the present, is quite a different thing to consumer immersion.

Nineteenth Sunday of the Year

1 Kings 19:9, 11–13; Romans 9:1–5; Matthew 14:22–33

We all hanker for that definitive experience of God that will lift us out of the rut of our daily lives, clarify the direction we should take for the future and resolve those pressing and seemingly insoluble questions. There is nothing wrong with this; both the Old Testament and New Testament contain stories of those who encounter God, are freed from sin or sickness and find new purpose in their lives. Also, our desire is no doubt fueled in part by the promise of heaven. But, our readings for this Sunday sound a counter theme that we need to take into consideration. The encounter with God may not go according to expectations or hopes. But this kind of encounter seems to be just as important as the other; depending on where we are in our lives, it may be more important. Not the kind of experience we want perhaps but the one we need.

The story of Elijah's experience of God at Mount Horeb might have been expected to follow the one of Israel's encounter with God at Sinai/Horeb, where a spectacular *son et lumiere* is followed by the establishment of a privileged relationship with God in the covenant. Not so. God is present in 'a voice of thin silence/small voice of silence' (the NRSV has 'the sound of sheer silence'), signaling something unexpected and almost indescribable. Elijah steps forward to meet his God and is asked a question 'what are you doing here Elijah'? The prophet proclaims that he is the only faithful one left but is corrected by God who says there are five thousand who have not bowed the knee to Baal. Elijah receives commissions that he never gets to carry out and an instruction to anoint Elisha as his successor. It is a very intense and intimate encounter with God but it effectively signals the end of Elijah as prophet. Yet Elijah is celebrated as one of the great

Old Testament prophets because he accepts his place in God's scheme of things, however unpalatable and disappointing it might seem.

In the second reading, Paul pours out his sorrow over 'my brothers of Israel' to his Roman readers. It is a measure of how much Paul hoped that his own conversion and his preaching of the gospel might touch and convert his fellow Jews. But it was not to be. No doubt Paul was completely committed to the Gentile mission and saw it as his calling from God. But his success in this arena seems only to have heightened his sense of failure in the other. Did Paul hope that his work might be crowned by some dramatic breakthrough in his relations with his Jewish brothers and sisters? It did not happen. Paul had to be content to pray for them and hope for them, but without the satisfaction of seeing their 'conversion'. One's vocation is about fulfilling the purpose that God has for us, not about our personal satisfaction.

When we turn to the gospel passage, we find a somewhat similar theme to the first two readings. Peter asks to experience Jesus' power over water and is invited by Jesus to step out of the boat. The presence of divine power is there; Peter walks on the water. But the experience does not elevate Peter to another realm, beyond that of his fellow disciples. The same man who a few minutes before recoiled in fear before a ghost now walks towards that ghost. Walking with Jesus on land or water does not mean that one is magically transported beyond one's fears, hatreds, weaknesses or strengths. If anything, it sharpens one's awareness of these. In Peter's case it is fear; more than responding to Jesus' invitation to walk on water, he needs to respond to Jesus' words 'do not fear'. The experience challenges Peter and the disciples to face and overcome, not the forces of nature, but the things that make us afraid to live our lives fully as Christians with all their joys and sorrows, because we do not trust God completely.

A number of commentators hold that this passage was designed to send a message to the struggling early church which was beset with difficulties, persecution and fear (note the earlier version of this story in 8:23—27). Jesus is there to help them but they need to trust him completely, even when the powers set against them seem overwhelming. Those who, like Peter, fail are rebuked but as long as they cry to the Lord in their weakness—again, like Peter—Jesus will not abandon them. The story serves as a call to those who have fallen by the wayside to avail of God's mercy and walk again in company with the Lord.

Twentieth Sunday of the Year

Isaiah 56:1, 6–7; Romans 11:13–15, 29–32; Matthew 15:21–28

We 'insiders', the members of the church, the chosen people, tend to think our role and the role of the church is to reach 'outsiders' and convert them. Up to a point this is true but it can lead us to make some dangerous assumptions about ourselves as the insiders as well as the outsiders. We are the givers they are the receivers. Our readings for this Sunday, in my view, reverse the direction. Outsiders are portrayed as the privileged ones who, in God's scheme of things, have something important to offer the insiders. It provides a challenge and healthy counter to the tendency to become complacent or even arrogant.

Take the reading from Isaiah 56. According to modern critical scholarship, this text comes late in the developing corpus of material attached to the great eighth century BCE prophet Isaiah. It reflects the challenges associated with attempts at restoration of the Israelite/Jewish community after the exile. Contrary to another view in Ezra–Nehemiah of how the post–exilic community should be constituted, the passage in Isaiah claims that foreigners are as welcome as Israelites. No separation is required. Their sacrifices will be as acceptable to God as those of Israelites; in fact, this text claims, the restored temple is to be a house of prayer for all peoples. Those who were left behind by the Babylonians and those who returned from the Babylonian exile are challenged to see the foreigner (even Babylonians!) as precious in God's sight as themselves, the chosen people. Race, history, culture, geography are no longer barriers to inclusion: the only things required for membership of the chosen people are respect for the Sabbath and loyalty to the covenant. Is it surprising that the alternative view tended to win out? Look at our own history, in particular our relationship with Jews and other Christian denominations, at least until recent times.

In a way, one could say that Paul shares some of the sentiments expressed in the reading from Isaiah. His hope is that the success of his Gentile mission will cause at least some of his brother and sister Jews to change their attitude. The chosen people at times thought of themselves as the envy of the world, not so much because they had better qualities than others but because of what God had done on their behalf. As Moses predicts in Deuteronomy 4:6, when the nations see the impact of the gift of the Torah in the lives of Israel in the land they will exclaim 'Surely this great nation is a wise and discerning people!' In the same way, Paul hopes that when the Jews see what God has done for the Gentiles in Jesus Christ, they will become envious and seek to join this new fellowship. Those who were once regarded as outsiders will help to bring about the conversion of those who think of themselves as insiders. And insiders normally think they have no need of conversion!

This same theme is dramatically captured in the gospel account of Jesus and the Canaanite woman. The word Canaanite was often used to express the opposite of being Israelite. The ultimate outsider (the woman) encounters the ultimate insider (Jesus). The account, as presented by Matthew, is challenging even for the reader. Jesus acts and speaks as the ultimate insider, exclusively focused on his mission as a Jew to his Jewish people and how a foreigner like her has no right to what belongs to 'the children'—God's chosen ones.

Interpreters have wrestled with the seemingly cold and aloof attitude of Jesus and have proposed that he is testing her faith. I prefer to go the other way; namely, that Jesus knows her faith (that is why she is there) and wants its greatness to be revealed and celebrated, a faith that is in sharp contrast to the reaction of so many of his people. She is another example of that figure in the gospels (the centurion, the good Samaritan, the sinner, the tax gatherer) whose faith and honesty is a revelation to those around Jesus and to us who read the gospel. Insiders tend to think they have a right to things, this woman recognises that she has no rights, no claim on Jesus. She has to depend entirely on his mercy and is completely willing to do so: it is at this point that the ultimate insider shows that he is equally able to be at one with the outsider; where there is such faith the barriers of religion, race and culture fade away. The relationship of faith between her and Jesus means that she is showered with the same abundant gifts as those God has bestowed on the chosen people.

Twenty First Sunday of the Year

Isaiah 22:15, 19–23; Romans 11:33–36; Matthew 16:13–20

As I read the famous passage from Matthew's Gospel, there are seven statements that Jesus makes in reply to Peter's confession that 'you are the Christ, the son of the living God'. And within the context of the Bible seven is a perfect number. Each statement says something not only about Peter and his role but also about the church—hence about ourselves

The first statement is the proclamation that 'you are a happy man'. One might have expected Jesus to say, 'you are right' or 'you have spoken the truth'. No doubt this element is there but the use of the Greek *'makarios'* which is translated as 'happy' or 'blessed' suggests that in making this profession of faith, something has happened to Peter. Jesus is not implying that Peter has better insight than his companions or is quicker off the mark, but that he has been singled out by God and anyone who is singled out by God for God's work is blessed indeed. In short, it is about election but, as Deuteronomy 7 says, God did not choose Israel because it was better or bigger than other nations but because God loved Israel and had a particular purpose for it in the divine scheme of things. So it is with Peter, so it is with each one of us.

Jesus' second statement is about the revelation of 'my Father' and emphasises that there is no separation between Jesus and his Father. Where Jesus is, the Father is there too. When taken in conjunction with the first statement, it also enables us to see that the intimate presence of the Father does not lessen the fact that this is Peter's confession of faith. Rather, the grace of God enhances the humanity of Peter.

The third statement involves the change of name. By virtue of God's grace Simon, as in baptism, becomes a new man with a new name. The fourth statement links his new name with his unique vocation, to be the 'rock'. The confidence and trust that Jesus has in us human beings is astonishing particularly when compared with the lack of trust that we ourselves place in our fellow men and women. Each vocation is a sign of God's trust and confidence.

The fifth statement shifts the focus somewhat from Peter to the church's battle against the forces of evil. These seek to enslave people in sin but the church built on the 'rock' will provide a safe haven of freedom for all those within its gates. The metaphor of a rock and of an impregnable fortress with gates can create a somewhat static impression of the church and the vocation of Peter.

As if to provide a balance, the sixth statement shifts to a more active stance by providing Peter with the keys of the kingdom of heaven. He is empowered to step out confidently from the fortress, the forces of evil reduced to impotence, and lead the faithful to their ultimate goal, the gates of the kingdom of heaven. But this kingdom is not some distant place; in Matthew's Gospel the kingdom of heaven is a circumlocution for the presence of God. Peter and the church usher people, freed from slavery, into the freedom of the presence of God.

The final statement respects a key feature without which the vocation of Peter and the church would not be truly human—decisions will have to be made and they will have to be made for the whole church, otherwise the whole enterprise would grind to a paralyzing halt. No decisions made by Peter or everyone making their own. To give Peter and the church the confidence to make decisions that at times may be painful and difficult, Jesus promises that the decisions will be ratified in heaven. This does not mean that they will automatically be the best or perfect decisions. As Paul says, 'we see now as in a mirror, darkly'. But God accepts the honest decisions that the church and indeed any Christian makes because they are part of a vocation of discipleship, part of being remade in the image and likeness of God.

If this passage is lifted out of its context, it can give the impression that Peter and the church will live a charmed life. As we know from the gospels and Acts of the Apostles, and our own history, this is not the case. Our passage is immediately followed by the one in which Jesus reprimands Peter and calls him 'Satan'. To go from a rock to a Satan in a few verses is almost as amazing as the reverse—the trust and confidence that God places in us poor human beings. God should consult a counselor but, as Paul says 'who could ever know the mind of the Lord? Who could ever be his counselor?' Only a God who loves in a way that we cannot fathom can keep trusting and forgiving those who continually fail; we certainly cannot.

Twenty Second Sunday of the Year

Jeremiah 20:7–9; Romans 12:1–2; Matthew 16:21–27

As noted in the reflections for the previous Sunday, Peter goes from being the foundational rock of the church to Satan in one gospel scene. Perhaps he thought that as the rock he had a 'mandate' as we say to take charge of Jesus' life and mission, to do what was best for him. Jesus' rebuke is sharp and clear but he nevertheless takes Peter up the mountain of the transfiguration with James and John. Jesus does not give up on the ones he chooses, despite their blunders.

Jesus' commitment to Peter and the disciples is demonstrated in the way he follows up the rebuke with an instruction (torah) that addresses our desire to be in control—of our own life and the life of others. Our modern technological world can lead us to become absorbed, even obsessed, with the conviction that our scientific know-how and marvelous machines will enable us to secure our lives. My life expectancy can be estimated accurately as such-and-such, I will therefore work for a certain number of years after which I will retire with a sufficient amount of money. I will follow a particular life style that will ensure my health and longevity. There are effectively no unforeseen factors. The inevitability of death recedes into the distance

But, Jesus asks 'what, then, will a man gain if he wins the whole world and ruins his life?' Clearly, Jesus is talking about a different 'life' to the one that our modern world holds up as the model. And it is not just eternal life but life here and now; if not then why speak of the incarnational aspect of our discipleship? What kind of life then are we to pursue as Christians? An essential component of it is that each 'renounce himself and take up his cross and follow me'. The picture this evokes of Jesus' staggering along under the burden of his cross is the very antithesis of the modern picture of someone who is in control of his or her life. To all intents and purposes it appears as the ultimate human indignity, complete loss of control.

But in a paradoxical way Jesus' call allows—better, encourages—each disciple to exercise control and in two key ways. The first is that Jesus gives each the freedom to make a decision (a more biblical term than 'control'): as he says, 'If anyone wants to be a follower of mine, *let him* renounce himself'. Discipleship is therefore a call, a challenge, it is not imposed. The second is to be found in the reading from Paul's letter to the Romans where he urges them to offer their living bodies as a holy sacrifice. In effect, one takes control of one's life by handing it over to God. All human beings crave a full human life. The Christian claim is that by handing our lives over to God we gain a real human life, not the substitute that our world offers. As our media frequently reminds us in news and stories, this 'substitute' for a real life is so often full of anxiety, fear, and isolation—in short, slavery.

In contrast, Christian discipleship does not lead to slavery and death but to freedom and glory because the one who goes before us has smashed the cross of sin and enslavement, a cross that we are unable to bear by ourselves, so that we are now able to take up the cross that we can bear—the giving of our lives in the service of our brothers and sisters. The Bible does not shy away from the difficulties that this real human life may bring—read the passage from the book of Jeremiah where the prophet voices his pain at having to bear 'insult, derision, all day long'. But by shouldering this burden as part of our discipleship we are one with him whose cross became the sign of victory over all forms of enslavement.

Twenty Third Sunday of the Year

Ezekiel 33:7–9; Romans 13:8–10; Matthew 18:15–20

Everything that we humans do or say operates within a context. Without a context within which we can relate and assess things we would be completely lost—as many of us feel when we first arrive in a foreign country where the language and cultural context is quite different to ours. If we take on (for example, children in a family) or are assigned responsibilities (for example, being appointed a parish priest), we need to know the context in which these responsibilities operate. Another way of putting this might be to say that where there are responsibilities there are rights and vice-versa. God's instructions to Ezekiel in our first reading are about his responsibilities as a prophet—very much in the mould of the prophet as a preacher of Torah rather than a 'seer' of the future. His responsibilities are outlined but then, as is required in the human realm and as God understands only too well, the context or boundaries within which the responsibilities operate are outlined ('then he shall die for his sin, but you yourself will have saved your life').

Given that Ezekiel accepts the responsibilities, he has a right to know to what extent they oblige him. Otherwise we poor human beings are likely to be overwhelmed. Once the prophet has done his duty therefore by warning the sinner, the text implies that God will step in: the sinner will die but Ezekiel will save his life. It is a bit uncertain as to whether the theologian behind this text is appealing to what is called the reward—retribution schema (God will bless the good and punish the wicked) or the act—consequence schema (good acts have good consequences, bad acts bad ones: that's the way the world that God created operates). Either option is a faith claim and the great mistake is to try and prove it from experience: Job and Ecclesiastes warn us of our inability to do this.

If the book of Ezekiel deals with specific responsibilities, Paul in Romans sets up a general principle ('If you love your fellow men you have carried out all your obligations'). Yet Paul knows only too well that however noble this principle is, it needs to be rooted in specific actions (as in the book of Ezekiel), otherwise his readers will not have an appropriate context. In a typical Pauline flourish, he meets the need for something specific by listing the commandments and then shows that by keeping each one of them his readers are fulfilling the general principle. He cannot be faulted because the general command to 'love your neighbour' is in the Torah along with specific commands (cf Leviticus 19:18). The limitation of the theology in Ezekiel is that one may equate righteousness with fulfilling obligations. Paul does not throw away the notion of obligation because it is too central to the gospel: we are commanded to love (be loyal to) our neighbour as we love God. However, he proclaims that this love of our neighbour, guided by the commands, should have a deep and unpayable debt as its goal: the debt (dependence may be a better translation) of mutual love. We human beings love to be in control, even when doing good to others. According to Paul, this is not what it is about, we should end up being happily dependent on the love of those to whom we have done good (as brothers and sisters of Christ) rather than exercise control over them by having them ever dependent on us.

As I read the gospel passage from Matthew, Jesus initially seems to follow the Ezekiel model by outlining one's responsibilities to one's brother and then by setting boundaries (the three occurrences of 'if he refuses to listen'). But it is the final phrase that catches my attention: 'treat him like a pagan or a tax collector'. This is quite different to Ezekiel's 'he shall die for his sin'. When one looks at the larger context of Matthew's Gospel, Jesus' instruction in this matter becomes clearer and it effectively blows out of the water any neat notion of boundaries in our responsibilities towards our neighbour. First, Matthew (one of Jesus' apostles and the traditional author of or figure behind the gospel) is a tax collector—how did Jesus treat him? He called him to discipleship. Second, at the end of the gospel Jesus instructs his disciples not to reject pagans (same basic Greek word as in 18:20) but to invite them to become children of God through baptism. It looks as though Jesus is admonishing us never to 'close the case' on anyone who is in conflict with the church community. No rejection can be regarded as final; at least not in this life. We are meant to be disciples of Christ and Jesus never gives up on any of his sheep, particularly the lost ones.

Twenty Fourth Sunday of the Year

Ecclesiasticus 27:30—28:7; Romans 14:7–9; Matthew 18:21–35

Our readings tackle the relationship between a duo that is foundational for our lives: justice and mercy/forgiveness. According to the Bible we cannot have one without the other and we would not need either if there was no sin. As far as I can tell we will not need justice and mercy in heaven because we will finally be graced to love as God loves. Like the other virtues such as faith, hope, courage, etc, justice and mercy will be perfected in perfect love.

Justice is needed to rectify our injustice towards our neighbour and even ourselves in this life; and the same goes for forgiveness. God is of course just and merciful and could not, by definition be anything else. In God they are one with God's love, goodness and truth. But, the reality of human sin and injustice and God's intervention against the 'sin of the world' reveals them as two sides as it were of one coin. We need a just God to judge where sin and injustice has occurred otherwise we would have no hope—says the Bible—of sorting out our relationships with God or with one another. We often still make a mess of it, despite the Bible and revelation. Once injustice in a relationship has been identified and its perpetrator has acknowledged the wrong then the relationship can be restored to its just state through pardon/forgiveness. Hence there can be no mercy without justice; that is, a judgment that wrong has been committed must first be made, and the relationship must be restored in a proper or righteous way. Similarly, there can be no justice without mercy which seeks to heal what has been wounded, to restore what has been damaged and divided. The relationship between justice and mercy/forgiveness is so close that we can easily miss one or confuse one with the other. This often occurs in our law courts where, despite the best intentions of law makers, the process of litigation results in divisions and barriers between the parties rather than the restoration of just relationships. One is convicted and taken to prison; the other is freed and, as often happens now, takes the money.

The reading from Ecclesiasticus or, in Hebrew, Ben Sirach can be read as a poetic presentation of rights and responsibilities within the context of Israel's covenant relationship. The passage ends with the ringing call to the reader/listener to 'remember the covenant of the Most High'. Within this covenant you enjoy the right to God's justice and mercy. You therefore have a responsibility to ensure that others enjoy the same rights. The 'neighbour' here in the Old Testament context would I think refer to another Israelite rather than include the foreigner. The implication of course is that it can be extended to include all kinds of neighbours. To treat your neighbour in the manner described is therefore not only a breach of covenant rights and responsibilities but an insult to God. A bit like a person who flouts all the rules of a club and is then outraged when he or she is given the boot. An important feature of this reading is that it shows the commandments are meant to serve and enhance justice and mercy/forgiveness ('remember the commandments, and do not bear your neighbour ill will'). There is no legalism here.

The gospel reading does much the same thing via a parable that contrasts a just and merciful king with his unjust and unforgiving servant. The gracious mercy of the king should have led to the servant being as merciful towards his fellow servant, his neighbour, but it didn't. This adds an element to the theology of Ben Sirach and it is the sober warning that experiencing forgiveness may not change me, the servant. I may be just as unforgiving afterwards as before. How to avoid this? One way is to listen to this kind of parable; it is a torah or teaching that a just and merciful Jesus provides to help us avoid falling into such a bleak hole. A key component of this teaching is that we are only able to forgive because God has first forgiven us. This forgiveness is of course dependent on our acknowledgment of our sins (God's judgment); if we do not acknowledge any sin how can there be forgiveness because, from our perspective, there is nothing to forgive or ask forgiveness for. How will I know that the grace of God's forgiveness has changed or is changing me? When I forgive my neighbour from my heart.

The reading from Paul adds another important ingredient to the justice–mercy nexus, namely that 'The life and death of each of us has its influence on others'. Paul is speaking primarily of the Christian community, the 'body of Christ' ('we live for the Lord') but it applies equally to the larger context of our 'global village'. When two people fall out there is a much wider ripple effect. The gospel parable catches this with its reference to the distress that the servant's conduct caused his fellow servants.

Twenty Fifth Sunday of the Year

Isaiah 55:6–9; Philippians 1:20–24, 27; Matthew 20:1–16

A clue to how one might read this Sunday's Gospel passage from Matthew lies in the final sentence: 'Thus the last will be first and the first, last'. As a comment on the parable that Jesus has just told, it implies that God will overturn human expectations and rankings—something that we all indulge in at one time or other. What is interesting is that this comment effectively repeats the one that Jesus makes at the end of the preceding chapter. When Peter asks him what 'we' who have left everything will get Jesus assures the twelve that they will be richly rewarded for their loyalty by being given a privileged position in the kingdom (judges). What is more, all those who have left all for the sake of Jesus' name will be richly rewarded. The chapter ends with Jesus saying 'But many who are first will be last, and the last will be first'. Is this a veiled warning against assuming that in becoming a disciple one has thereby *left everything* and so is entitled to the reward? Perhaps the presence of this saying before and after the parable is inviting us to read it in relation to those who are disciples and those who are perceived as outside.

The workers who are engaged early in the day (about 6 am) have an agreement or promise with their boss about their pay, the reward of their labours (so Peter and the apostles). Other workers are hired throughout the day, at 9am, 12noon, 3pm and finally at 5pm. Significantly, the parable is really only concerned with the relationship between the 'last comers' and those we might call the 'early birds' and this suggests a link to the topic of the preceding discourse and the saying about the first and the last. The last comers receive the same amount (reward) from the boss as the early birds. At this point in the parable we have its three key players: early birds, last comers and the boss and we are invited to think about each within the context of Matthew's Gospel.

Let us start with the boss—God. It is significant that God keeps going out to look for workers, even at the last hour. What is the point of this? You do not take on staff just as you are about to close the shop for the day and just because they have not been employed. It is not good business sense, and it is even worse business sense to pay them a full day's wages. Such a business will either go broke or is being run on quite different lines and the boss has resources well beyond our reckoning, with a different attitude to the normal ones.

Next we turn to the last comers. From their point of view they were about to miss out on work, and here they are spending a brief period in the vineyard yet getting full pay. How many times have we heard people lament that they have left it too late to be reconciled to God or to make something of their life? This parable teaches that we can never be too late with God, or too early. The prophecy from Isaiah shares this theology, assuring sinners not to think that it is too late, that it is all over between them and God. The mistake is to transfer their sense of being too late onto God but, as the prophecy says, 'my thoughts are not your thoughts, my ways not your ways'. For God one moment of repentance reaps a full reward because 'our God is rich in forgiving', a generous God as the parable makes clear. This is the sense in which we can truly say that a moment becomes an eternity.

As for the early birds, their mistake is to think that time spent on the job is the main thing rather than being chosen for the job. It is good to celebrate long loyal service and jubilees as long as these do not lead us to think that these win God's love in return. We can only love God because God has first loved us, has chosen us. Our love of God is a consequence of being loved by God, not a pre-requisite for it. What the early birds and the last comers share, and what should unite them, is that both have been chosen to work in the vineyard.

In being so chosen, each worker should be willing to do things God's way because it will be the best way. This can take some learning. In the reading from Philippians Paul admits that he is caught between two desires. One (and it seems to be the principal one) is to be free of this world and to be one with Christ in the resurrection. This would bring about his perfection and, after all, this is what Christ desires for him. But his perfection involves being 'like Christ' who gave himself in the service of others. Hence, an integral part of Paul being made perfect is doing what Jesus did and desiring to do it as well as he can—serving his brothers and sisters faithfully. If it is Christ's will that he remain 'in this body' to continue working as a disciple, then so be it. Paul is honest, admitting that he cannot set aside his own self-interest while serving his brothers and sisters. But he is content to live with unresolved tension and leave its resolution in God's hands. We talk about selfless service and it is a great ideal, but can we—indeed should we—ever claim to act without self-interest? As Jesus says, 'you shall love your neighbour as you love yourself'.

Twenty Sixth Sunday of the Year

Ezekiel 18:25–28; Philippians 2:1–11 or 2:1–5;
Matthew 21:28–32

We like to think that we are adaptable, open to change and ready to make it, the most innovative people in history. Maybe. I tend to think that we are pretty much the same as people throughout history. Like them we resist change unless it is on our terms and to our advantage. There lies the rub. What kind of change is really to our advantage? We need to have a critical or informed attitude about change. After all, change of itself is not necessarily a good thing. Our readings for this Sunday provide food for thought on what kind of changes we need to make.

In the first reading, Ezekiel is in vigorous debate about a traditional proverbial saying or jibe that is quoted at the beginning of chapter 18: 'the fathers have eaten sour grapes and the children's teeth are set on edge'. The same quote occurs in Jeremiah 31:29. The fact that it is taken up by two major prophetic books suggests it was a hot topic during and after the exile, when it is believed the books of Jeremiah and Ezekiel were compiled. Ezekiel quotes the saying in order to refute it by teaching that each person (and each generation) is responsible for his or her sin and must bear the consequences. In this way, he defends God's justice against his opponents' accusation and at the end of the chapter urges them to change their theology and their wicked ways. What are their wicked ways? Rather clever ones, as I read the passage, but Ezekiel is on to them. They are appealing to the saying on two counts in order to avoid the challenge of change. Both involve playing the old blame game, putting God in the dock. On the one hand, they say 'why should we be just, indeed how can we be expected to be just, when God is unjust'? On the other hand they say 'don't blame me for what happens to the kids; that's the way this unjust God has set things up'. Even though they mock the theology behind the saying, in fact it suits them very well: no need to change at all. This attitude is a bit like voting to keep in the politicians that we love to hate.

In the Gospel passage from Matthew, Jesus deftly turns the correct response of his adversaries into a challenge that they are reluctant to take on board. When asked the question about the little parable that he tells, the chief priests and elders identify the son who made the good change as the one 'who did the father's will'. At this point we need to remember that in the preceding scene in the temple the same chief priests and elders challenge Jesus about his authority to teach. For them, the good and necessary change is for others—particularly troublesome characters like Jesus—to become like them. As they are portrayed in Matthew's Gospel, which is all we know about them, the chief priests and elders see themselves as loyal to the Torah and tradition. But Jesus turns the tables on them by identifying the very ones they reject—the tax collectors and prostitutes—as the ones who make the right changes. They responded to the teachings of the righteous John the Baptist but when the priests and elders saw this, they 'refused to think better of it (sic. change) and believe in him'. Given their assumption that everyone should move in their direction, they see no need for change and it is therefore unthinkable for them (say 'impossible') to take up Jesus' challenge to follow the example of tax collectors and prostitutes.

The passage from Paul's letter to the Philippians with its famous christological hymn outlines very nicely the kind of changes that we as Christians need to make. As a wise teacher, Paul outlines the challenge and then provides a portrait of Christ as our model. The hymn presents Jesus as the model of change: he emptied himself and became a servant of all. This did not involve the master 'playing the role' of a servant: the master *became* the servant and submitted to the most challenging change any human being will face—death, and the most momentous change that we will ever undergo—resurrection. Jesus undertook these changes, not because he needed to be made perfect, but in order to show us how to become perfect: it is for our sakes as the conclusion to the hymn indicates.

When Paul urges his community at Phillipi to have 'a common purpose and a common mind' he does not mean that they are all to become clones of one another. Far from it. Being conformed to our model Jesus means for Paul that we become fully what we are meant to be, what we really desire—fully human both as individuals and as community. What is the sign that we are on the road to achieving these changes? In the words of the letter, the sign is that 'nobody thinks of his own interests first but everybody thinks of other people's interests instead'. This kind of change is beyond us mere mortals, as the Gospel passage from Matthew suggests. It can only come about as the result of the grace or gift that Christ bestows on his disciples. It is this alone that enables us to make the right changes to our life.

Twenty Seventh Sunday of the Year

Isaiah 5:1–7; Philippians 4:6–9; Matthew 21:33–43

The texts from Isaiah and Matthew show how an inspired mind can take the common rustic image of a vineyard and turn it into a powerful prophetic message. In Isaiah, the poetic account of how God planted a vineyard, cared for it and did everything for it is effectively a review of God's dealings with his people. There is nothing particularly new in this; it is a common enough ploy in prophetic preaching, designed to defend the justice and goodness of God in comparison to the evils committed by God's people. God cannot be blamed for the evils in society. Where the crunch comes is the following piece of the prophecy. It proclaims what God will do to the vineyard and, for any person with minimal knowledge of agricultural practice, it is disturbing news. What vintner in his right mind would let the investment that he lavished so much care on go to rack and ruin? An incompetent farmer to say the least. What is even more disturbing, Isaiah claims that God will do the same to the chosen people—why? Because the divine purpose driving this massive investment is something more foundational and important than Israel or Judah and if God cannot get a decent return on the investment through these chosen agents, then God will do it another way, so obsessed is the divinity with this purpose. What is God's driving purpose? The last part of the reading reveals it: justice and righteousness/integrity.

This would have been a shocking text to Isaiah's listeners and no doubt it was meant to make them take notice and think and hopefully change. As the book unfolds, the hope is expressed that Israel will one day be able to fulfill its God–given mission. Isaiah 2:1–4 prophesies that one day Zion will become a beacon of God's justice and peace for all the nations. By then Israel (and you the reader of the book) will know not to condemn others who fail because God has forgiven it for its failures.

Matthew's version turns the well-known image into an equally powerful and challenging message, but in a somewhat different way to Isaiah. What strikes me when reading this passage is how the explanation of key aspects of the parable is withheld until almost the last moment. In a real sense, the last line is the crunch line. As we listen to the parable, we are not sure who or what is the vineyard. In the Isaiah version the vineyard is the 'house of Israel' and the men of Judah God's 'pleasant planting'. In Matthew's version, we learn right at the end that the vineyard is nothing less than the kingdom of God; for Matthew this is the presence of God. The kingdom of God is not something that you can seize like an inheritance; it is gift. We quite understandably think that the wicked tenants kill the servants because they want the produce for themselves. The chief priests and elders certainly read it this way. We are surprised and perhaps even shocked to learn that there was no produce to take. The tenants had done nothing with the vineyard and that is why it will be given to 'a people who will produce its fruit'. We understandably identify the 'son' in the parable as a reference to Jesus. But Jesus, as the narrator of the parable, springs another surprise by shifting our focus from the evil done to the son to 'a people' to whom the vineyard will be given. The preceding quote from Psalm 117/118 hints that this people are not the ones you would expect to end up tenants of a vineyard but God 'prophesies' that they will produce the fruit that the 'chosen' ones failed to produce.

What is the marvelous fruit of this vineyard that is the kingdom of God? For an answer I think we can invoke both Isaiah and Paul. In the words of Isaiah it is justice and righteousness. In the words of Paul it is 'everything that is true, everything that is noble, everything that is good and pure, everything that we love and honour, and everything that can be thought virtuous or worthy of praise'. 'Fill your minds' with this fruit, Paul recommends and 'the God of peace will be with you' because the kingdom of God is among you.

God entrusted the kingdom of God on earth to Israel and looked to it to produce the fruit of this kingdom: a community of justice, righteousness and peace. The harsh claim is that there has been no such fruit. According to this text, the chief priests and elders are warned that the kingdom will be entrusted to a people, an unlikely people from their point of view, who will produce its fruit. As God trusted Israel, so God will trust this people. We in the church like to think we are that people. As disciples of Jesus we can make the claim but that means we also, like Israel, must take on board the responsibility that goes with being custodians of the kingdom. Have we been any better in living up to the trust that has been placed in us? Thank God for a merciful God.

Twenty Eighth Sunday of the Year

Isaiah 25:6–10; Philippians 4:12–14, 19–20;
Matthew 22:1–14 or 22:1–10

The biblical tradition liked the image of a great feast to communicate something of its conviction about the ultimate purpose of God. The passage from Isaiah paints a portrait of the final festal banquet around two key notions of God: the utterly transcendent one who is also the utterly immanent one. Only the utterly transcendent one can prepare a banquet for all peoples that is utterly lavish and generous. Only the utterly transcendent God can remove the mourning veil covering all peoples of every time and place. By the same token, only the utterly immanent God can personally wipe away the tears 'from ever cheek'. A God who is utterly transcendent can at the same time be utterly immanent and vice-versa. The ultimate purpose of this marvelous banquet is that all will recognise that 'this is our God'. According to the Bible, God acts so that the reality and glory of God will be manifest in creation and acknowledged by humanity. It is only on the basis of this that everything else can find its proper places—our relationships with God, with one another, with creation, etc.

The Gospel passage from Matthew addresses a key stage before the final realization of God's purpose via the parable of the wedding feast—the invitation to come. Those first invited initially refuse and subsequently abuse the king's servants. The two groups of servants could refer to the Old Testament prophets or to a combination of the Old Testament prophets and the New Testament disciples of Jesus. Parables leave things open and invite listeners/readers to fill in the 'gaps'. What is striking about this parable however is that on hearing of the abuse of his servants, the king suspends all preparations for the wedding for his son and deals with those who abused and killed his servants. Some find this a strange intrusion in the parable but, as I read it, it signals that the king regards his servants as equally precious as his son. They are not second class, disposable 'servants'. Hence the king devotes as much energy to righting the awful wrong perpetrated against his servants as he has devoted to the wedding of his son. Another angle on the transcendent and immanent? Whatever the case, there is a strong message for the 'servants' of the king who proclaims this parable. Their suffering will not be forgotten, will not be in vain. Justice for all is an integral part of the king's preparation for the great feast.

After righting this wrong, the king invites all and sundry to his wedding; good and bad alike. God's invitation does not depend on how good you are beforehand; God loves all and all are precious in God's sight. But, one cannot assume to enter the wedding banquet on one's own terms, without any change at all. The episode of the person failing to don a wedding garment implies that he sees no difference at all between being outside or inside the wedding hall as an honoured guest. Or, even worse, he is deliberately demeaning its significance. The episode adds an important element to the theology of the festal banquet: it is not so much about a party but about our transformation, our being made perfect. We are all invited as we are so that we may become what God wants us to be. And this will be to the glory of God.

On a first reading, one might think that Paul's statement in his letter to the Philippians is rather presumptuous: this is a man who thinks he is perfect, who knows what it is all about ('there is nothing I cannot master'). Two statements in the passage save Paul from such an accusation. The first is his acknowledgment that anything he does is done 'with the help of the One who gives me strength'. Without that strength, Paul knows how weak and helpless he is. The second is his interest in the welfare of his helpers rather than his own. It was good that they came to help him in his troubles and he thanks them for that. But, more importantly, he gives thanks that this good act of theirs shows how much they are imbued with the Christian spirit. It is a sign that God 'will fulfill all your needs, in Christ Jesus, as lavishly as only God can'. In a word, they are not far from that final, eschatological, lavish banquet.

Twenty Ninth Sunday of the Year

Isaiah 45:1, 4–6; 1 Thessalonians 1:1–5; Matthew 22:15–21

Our readings for this Sunday provide an opportunity to reflect on something that is central to our faith—the Word of God. Each reading offers an angle on the mystery of the word of God and each angle challenges and surprises. The surprising thing about the reading from Isaiah is that the Word of God is addressed to the Persian conqueror Cyrus, the ultimate outsider. Even though Cyrus does not know the God of Israel, this is no barrier. God calls him personally by name as he called Moses and gives him the title of Messiah or anointed one, the only foreigner in the Old Testament to be given this title and the only figure in the book of Isaiah to be so described. Not even the Immanuel to come in Isaiah 9 and 11 is called Messiah. And, like David, Cyrus is given a commission to deliver Israel from oppression. In a way, this outsider becomes a favoured insider, Israel's deliverer personally called and commissioned by God. This may have come as something of a shock to the insiders, the Judean exiles in Babylon. To the outsiders, whether Persian or Babylonian, it would probably have appeared outrageous, even laughable.

Cyrus's vocation is not simply to deliver Israel. In a further challenge to established categories of thinking, the prophecy proclaims that God has a purpose in this that goes beyond Israel: it is that all may come to know that 'apart from me, all is nothing'. God's ultimate purpose is that people come to acknowledge the reality of God. Only on this basis can everything else fall into place.

The First Letter to the Thessalonians is believed to be Paul's first and therefore probably reflects the early stages of his preaching mission. In reading our passage, one senses Paul's wonder and delight at the impact that the preaching of the Good News had on the Thessalonians. What astonishes him is the realisation that the preaching of the Good News is not just the communication of a message, a word. It is a personal presence of the Holy Spirit and an encounter with the Spirit. The presence of the Holy Spirit is encountered in two ways. On the one hand it inspires those preaching the Good News; on the other hand it empowers those who hear the Good News. There are times when being in the presence of a speaker is uplifting and empowering, and it is not just because of his or her words. The words mediate a personal encounter and one knows deep down that being in the presence of this person is a life-giving, privileged moment.

In the Gospel passage from Matthew we encounter the Word himself in debate with the Pharisees. Two things—at least—are surprising and challenging about the behaviour of the incarnate Word in this scene. The first is that although Jesus knows the deceptive motive behind their question and points this out to them bluntly, he does not dismiss them or walk away. The Good News is preached even to those with evil intent who have thereby placed themselves on the outside ('I have come to call the sinners, not the virtuous'). This suggests that the message or response that Jesus makes is important. But, as one reads it, there is another surprise. The Incarnate Word does not appear to answer the pressing question whether a Jew should pay taxes to the foreign overlord. He seems to leave the decision up to them. This may be meant to indicate that Jesus comes to challenge us to make decisions about our life, not to provide a ready list of solutions to every question that we raise or problem that we encounter. In short, the Word challenges us to speak our word and act on it.

But, a closer look at the passage prompts another interpretation. Jesus prefaces his reply by asking the Pharisees whose image is on the coin. Those things that bear the image of Caesar belong to Caesar and, by implication, those things that bear the image of God belong to God. What in the context of this passage bears the image of God? Surely it is the Pharisees and indeed all human beings. On this reading, Jesus' word is a challenge, an invitation to his questioners, to look at themselves from another angle, not as subjects who willingly or unwillingly use the Roman system, but who they really are despite their flaws—the image and likeness of God. If only they could 'see' that the pure image and likeness of God is the one speaking to them, then they might be able to look at themselves from his perspective.

Thirtieth Sunday of the Year

Exodus 22:20–26; 1 Thessalonians 1:5–10; Matthew 22:34–40

Jesus' reply to the Sadducees in today's Gospel from Matthew draws together two separate commands in the Old Testament Torah. The command to love God occurs in Deuteronomy 6:5 and is part of the famous '*shema*' (hear O Israel!) prayer that is recited in the synagogue every Sabbath. The command to love one's neighbour is in Leviticus 19:18. This pithy Gospel from Matthew packs a lot of punch. Three reactions or questions spring to mind (for a start). Why does God command us to love? We speak of 'falling in love'; do you ever hear our governments commanding people to love? If they did it would be greeted with incredulity or seen as a gross intrusion of privacy. Why does Jesus combine these two commands in response to the Sadducees' question about the one greatest command? Thirdly, why does the second one command us to love our neighbour as we love ourselves? It almost looks as though there are two commands here. We are commanded to love our neighbour and to love ourselves. The gospel implies that if we do not love ourselves then it is unlikely we will be able to love our neighbour or even to love God.

In answer to the first question, we can take a lead from the text in Deuteronomy that follows the command to love God. It commands Israelites to 'keep' the words of the Torah in their hearts, in other words to be completely loyal to it. How is this loyalty manifested? By teaching one's children about the Torah, by talking about it at key points in the day, and by visibly displaying one's commitment to it. For the Torah, love of God means loyalty to God according to the instructions or guidelines that God has provided. These instructions are about what one is to do, not how one is to feel about God or neighbour. If one feels good about God that is a plus but the Torah knows feelings and emotions cannot be commanded. The biblical notion of love is rather different to our romantic one.

As for the second question, we can take a lead from the Decalogue or Ten Commandments where commands about loyalty to God are followed by commands about loyalty to neighbour. The implication here is that one who worships the God of Israel will therefore be loyal to his/her neighbour according to the Decalogue. If not, then one's love of God is a sham. Or, if one starts from the laws about neighbour in the Decalogue then I love my neighbour according to these laws primarily because I love (am loyal) God who established the covenant relationship and these laws. These in turn reveal God's love for my neighbour and for me. What greater reason or motivation can I therefore have for loving my neighbour? Moreover, the command challenges me to see my neighbour from God's true perspective rather than my own warped one. That the Torah regards one's love of neighbour as a sign of one's love of God is abundantly clear in the first reading from Exodus. The severe punishment threatened in this law suggests that the theologians who drafted it found it hard to imagine that a person who claims to love God would do such things to a neighbour whom God loves.

In relation to the third question, one could reply that the text is not commanding us to love ourselves, rather it assumes that we love ourselves. Hence this command is another version of 'do unto others as you would want them to do unto you'. However, I prefer to see it as a command that issues the same challenge about how I should see myself as I should see my neighbour—and act accordingly. That is, I should be loyal to my true self because I love God who is the one above all who knows my true self and loves me unconditionally, despite my flaws and failures. Again, what better reason or motivation is there for loving oneself?

When reflecting on these commands to love it is well to keep in mind the covenant context in which they occur. According to the Torah, God establishes the covenant relationship because God loves Israel. In response to this divine initiative, Israel it called to love God and neighbour. To put this another way, we are called to love because God has first loved us. We are called to give but we can only give what we have first received.

Some might think that being 'receivers' and obeying commands cripples one's individuality and creativity. Not so, says Paul in the second reading. The Thessalonians indeed began by being imitators (how else does one begin) but they in turn became 'a great example to all' by their own unique response to persecution and opposition. The imitators themselves have become worthy of imitation. The gift of God's love is creative and liberating. Paul only 'started the work' among them, they then developed it in a way that radically changed their lives.

Thirty First Sunday of the Year

Malachi 1:14–2:2, 8–10; 1 Thessalonians 2:7–9, 13;
Matthew 23:1–12

We all need authority in our lives and these readings can help us get some things right about it and how it should be exercised. Our English word comes from the Latin *auctoritas*—source or origin. An *'auctor'* or author begins or originates something. The reason we all need authority is at base very simple: we are not the originators of our lives and, generally, we do not end them. As well as this, we have to rely on authorities (*auctores*) for our life's journey: we are limited human beings and cannot monitor or assess all the phenomena of a single life, let alone humanity and its history. Authority therefore involves faith: in order to live we have to trust the information and judgment of others in a host of areas.

The Bible claims that the only one who is able to monitor and assess everything in creation is God because God, being outside creation, can 'see' it all. Because God is the only true *'auctor'* or author of life we are all God's sons and daughters. Therefore, we should treat one another as brothers and sisters. This is what Jesus teaches in the reading from Matthew and what the reading from Malachi appeals to: 'Have we not all one Father?' It seems so obvious that everyone will see it and act accordingly, but of course we don't. Why not?

One reason, within the Jewish–Christian tradition, is the Bible's teaching that God acts through intermediaries to whom authority is delegated. God does not impose this mediation, it is an invitation and challenge to which people are free to respond. If it was imposed then it would not be biblical. Hence hierarchy or structure is an integral part of the Bible message. But once you bring temptation prone authority figures into contact with temptation prone subjects then things can go wrong. The call to true freedom within the context of God's law can be skewed by the figures in authority; the response to the call can be skewed by a distorted perception of freedom. The passages from Malachi and from Matthew charge the figures in authority with abuse of their role but there are other passages in the Bible that are equally critical of the people. In both Malachi and Matthew the charge is that the delegated authorities have not only failed to represent their authority, God, but they have distorted God's message as well. The passage in Malachi issues a warning to the priests as if there is still time to repent and change: 'if you do not find it in your heart to glorify my name'. In contrast Jesus sees that the distortion perpetrated by the scribes and Pharisees is so bad people need to be warned about it: 'do not be guided by what they do; since they do not practice what they preach'.

The reading from Paul's letter to the Thessalonians provides the model by which all authority figures in the community should operate. Attitude is a key: Paul and his co-workers came to Thessalonica not to dominate but to love (and love is always free), not to take but to give (to hand over to you not only the Good New but our whole lives as well). They were able to do this not because of winning qualities in themselves but because of the grace of Christ working through them. What Paul is really relieved about is that the Thessalonians heard their preaching as 'God's message' rather than their own thoughts and words. This means that, thanks again to the grace of Christ, their presence and their work pointed not to themselves but to Christ, the true 'author' of all that they did.

The point of the readings may be enhanced a little if we compare their notion of authority with alternatives that humanity has tried over the centuries. One is the individual who claims to be the source of all authority—whether it be king, tyrant, priest, prophet or 'president for life' figures. The claim is illogical because this person is just another human being after all, not a true '*auctor*'. Another is the group or party that takes control and claims all authority, modern examples being Nazism/Fascism and Communism. Even though these movements mouth the slogans that 'we are all brothers and sisters', the reality is generally the complete opposite. Members of the party may enjoy some brotherly and sisterly status, the rest are merely servants of the machine. The third is the very modern one of the individual who does not wish to impose on anyone else or be responsible to anyone else. This person claims to exercise authority only over his or her own life. This may be well intentioned but in my judgment it too is illogical as well as unreal. Not only does it suffer from the same flaw that a person is not his or her own '*auctor*', but one can only be an individual

'I' by contrasting oneself with others who are not 'I'. The others are there whether an individual likes it or not and it is unreal and dangerous to try and ignore them. The individual will have an impact on others and vice versa. In contrast, the Christian attitude should be: our greatest dignity is to live as creatures of our creator, our greatest temptation is to try and become creator.

Thirty Second Sunday of the Year

Wisdom 6:12–16; 1 Thessalonians 4:13–18; Matthew 25:1–13

There are a number of passages in the gospels in which Jesus exhorts the disciples to 'stay awake' because he will come at an hour they do not expect. The lectionary selects a number of these passages for the Sundays leading up to the end of the liturgical year. Reflection upon them in their respective contexts shows—to me at least—that they are not all to be understood in the same sense. The call to 'stay awake' can take on different shades of meaning depending on context and I comment on the other occurrences in their respective contexts. Like other treasured sayings of Jesus such as 'the kingdom of heaven', 'your faith has saved you', 'listen anyone who has ears to hear', it is an invitation and challenge to think about its meaning in this or that passage.

What then of its occurrence in the famous parable of the bridesmaids with their lamps? A clue to how to read the command to 'stay awake' is that all ten had a good nap while they waited for the bridegroom's arrival. The point of the parable therefore is not to literally stay awake because this would mean censure for the wise bridesmaids as well as the foolish ones. The mention of 'wise' provides a second clue to the meaning of staying awake. The wise ones had made the best preparations they could for the climax or purpose of their role as bridesmaids: being ready to accompany the bridal party (even though they had fallen asleep as they waited). Translate the parable into the language of Christian vocation and it is designed to remind us of our complete dependence on God our beginning and our goal. If we have this perspective we are wise indeed and well prepared for whatever eventuates.

Talk of being wise turns our attention to the first reading from the book of Wisdom. We can see here an Old Testament version of the play on the meaning of words and phrases that characterises a number of Jesus' sayings in the gospels. This is a very late book in the pre-Christian Jewish tradition and written in Greek (it is in not in the Hebrew canon or list of sacred writings). But it has the advantage of being able to draw on a wealth of Jewish tradition that reflected on divine Wisdom in the guise (as a metaphor) of a woman. The writer lavishly celebrates the benefits of Wisdom but there are a number of important caveats that caution those who think they may have it or perhaps have been disappointed in their search for it. The first is that one must love her; then she will be found. But when can you say you truly love wisdom? An invitation to reflection. The second is that one must watch for her early, which may well mean that learning wisdom from God involves a life-long commitment. There is no crash course in it. Finally, the writer claims that Wisdom seeks 'those who are worthy of her', but who would claim to be worthy? Perhaps to proclaim one's unworthiness is a sign of being worthy in the eyes of Wisdom.

While this writer is rightly celebrating the importance of wisdom he is gently but firmly hosing down expectations that it provides ready answers or quick fixes. He is too immersed in his tradition and the lesson of his own experience to think there are ready made answers. Perhaps the author of Psalm 73 catches the Old Testament attitude to wisdom well. This is a psalm by a person who after a long and bitter search for answers that would explain and satisfy his questions about good and evil came to see that the most important thing was the faith conviction that 'my flesh and my heart may fail, but God is the strength of my heart and my portion forever' (NRSV translation). Psalm 63:3 says simply yet powerfully 'your steadfast love is better than life'.

The passage from 1 Thessalonians (Paul's first letter) provides another angle on staying awake. Understandably, there was a strong expectation in the early church that the 'second coming' of Jesus would occur soon. This led to the conviction among some that those 'awake' at the time would be better off—they would see Jesus in his glory and receive their reward as he promised. Did this mean that the death of members of the community in the 'between time' was some sign of failure on their part as Christians or a judgment against them? It seems members of the community were worrying and grieving about their dead. Paul seeks to ease their anxiety by assuring them that being 'awake' when the Lord comes is no advantage over those who have died. All will enjoy the resurrection, those who are 'awake' and watching when the Lord comes (that is, being faithful disciples according to their vocation) and the dead, as long as they 'died in Jesus' (that is, as long as they 'stayed awake' by being faithful disciples during their lives).

Thirty Third Sunday of the Year

Proverbs 31:10–13, 19–20, 30–31; 1 Thessalonians 5:1–6;
Matthew 25:14–30 or 25:14–15, 19–20

As I have noted before, parables are powerful but like all literary forms, they are limited. Every form or way of communicating provides us with an opportunity to be creative but imposes certain limitations. Parables tend to highlight one or two points and that is their power: they focus the mind. But once one shifts to a broader focus, gaps can start to appear that require explanation. That is why I think parables in the gospel are often presented in a collection or series in which one bounces off another. The preceding parable in Matthew 25 is about the bridesmaids who need to 'stay awake' in the sense of being wise about their preparations, otherwise they are likely to miss out on joining in the wedding celebrations. This kind of watchfulness focuses on the culmination or goal of the journey of faith. It is one of the aims and objects of contemplative prayer. But, it does raise a question about the relationship of the various stages of our journey to the goal (the Mary and Martha debate?), of how one's seemingly insignificant life contributes to God's plan. It can also imply that the bridesmaids are not part of the show until it gets under way with the arrival of the bridal party.

Our parable of the talents (a valuable unit of currency not a human skill) answers these kinds of questions. It highlights the contribution the servants are meant and able to make to the master's business while he is away. It is not their money but his; hence, they are busy on his behalf, not their own. Each one is given an amount 'according to his ability' (each vocation is unique). The master knows the ability (gifts or talents) of his servants but does not impose any conditions on them, any levels of achievement that need to be attained. They are entrusted with the money and that is that. The first two servants use their God-given skills, take risks and make decisions about something that is not their own. They are successful. An interesting implication in this—not explicit in the parable—is that they succeed as long as they are using their talents in the service of their master. The parable leaves open how one might apply this (because parables are meant to be applied to our lives), however one can reasonably say that it implies that God's community of believers and the spread of the gospel will increase. When the master returns for the reckoning, the faithful servants who put their lives in the service of their master's property now get to share the property. What was not theirs now becomes theirs. And what is this property that is now shared with them? Nothing less than the life of the master ('your master's happiness').

In contrast the third servant does nothing yet blames the master for effectively obliging him to do so. That is, he created an atmosphere of fear via his fearsome reputation. It is an attempt to take control of things and put the master on trial, to reverse the role of servant and master. The master who put complete faith in his servant according to his ability is accused of being untrustworthy. For the sake of truth (proved by the freedom and initiative shown by the other servants) and the welfare of the 'property', this false order must be exposed and the true order of things reestablished. We are God's trusted agents going about God's business. If we don't trust God in return or try to go about God's business on our terms then, the parable implies, we will make a mess of it. The business of salvation is so central and important God will not let it be hampered in this way. A passage from Nicholas Lash catches for me very succinctly the relationship between the parable of the bridesmaids and the parable of the talents; 'The distinction to be drawn lies not, I think, between action and passion, between "doing things" and having things done to one, but rather between behaving as if we were the centre of the world and learning that we are not'.[5]

Paul's letter about knowing 'times and seasons' can be read in the same vein. One who desires to know when the Lord will come is in danger of being untrusting and of seeking to be in control of things. If I know the 'day' then I can plan things to suit myself. I might think that this will help me to be better, to see things more clearly, but for Paul it is a sign that I am still in the dark, unwilling to be led out into the true light of day.

The reading from Proverbs provides yet another angle on our theme. In chapter 9, Lady Wisdom invites pupils to her school to learn wisdom

---

5   Nicholas Lash, sermon on 'Watchfulness' in *Seeing in the Dark: University Sermons* (London: Darton Longman & Todd, 2005) 23.

via the proverbs that follows in 10:1—31:9. Graduation as a wise person means 'marrying' Lady Wisdom, the perfect wife of course, as our passage affirms. By making her the centre of your life and being absolutely devoted to her teaching ('her husband's heart has confidence in her'), she makes you the centre of her life ('advantage . . . she brings him all the days of her life').

Our Lord Jesus Christ, Universal King

Ezekiel 34:11–12, 15–17;
1 Corinthians 15:20–26, 28; Matthew 25:31–46

The famous 'last judgment' picture painted by our text from Matthew evokes, and probably draws on, the grandeur of an ancient Near Eastern royal court. The sovereign, accompanied by a mightily impressive retinue, summons the vassal states (all the nations are assembled) to report on their conduct. On such occasions, as in our own times, the representatives of the nations have carefully prepared reports that will not only flatter their sovereign but also enhance their own standing. But, as we have found in the Bible, expectations tend to get turned upside down. Instead of being summoned to give their reports (recall the parable of the talents), the king here hands out rewards and punishments for things that shock and surprise both the sheep and the goats. In dramatic stories or scenes like these, someone or some animal has to stand in for all the wicked and here it is the goats. Goats fare somewhat better in the reading from Ezekiel and, according to Exodus 12:5, goats are just as acceptable as sheep for the Passover meal.

What strikes me about this Matthean text is that Jesus does not note how many times one has celebrated a liturgy in his honour and how grand or solemn they have been, Nor is there any mention of how many times one has praised him in song or asked him for favours. What he is primarily concerned about are the deprived members of his kingdom, and there seem to be plenty of them. Indeed, this kingdom sounds rather like the gospel's description of the Palestine province of the Roman empire in which Jesus carried out his ministry: full of the poor, the thirsty, the hungry, the naked, the sick, prisoners and strangers. Has anything changed?

Our text seems to imply that Jesus entrusted the kingdom to disciples (recall again the parable of the talents) in whom he had complete confidence. They were to give themselves completely in the service of any who were in need because this is the example that the king himself gave them. The king, the master, became the servant of all and gave himself for all those in need. It does not matter what family or nation or race they belong to; they are all part of Jesus' kingdom, his brothers and sisters, his family. We can see that the customary notion of a kingdom is being thoroughly rewritten by the gospels.

Jesus' disciples have been made kings and masters of his kingdom on earth: this means that they are to exercise their kingship by being servants of all, like Jesus. It does not mean that they play the role of a servant for a time and then revert to what they really prefer—being the masters. No, it means that they really become servants, something that only the grace of Christ can empower them (us) to become. Service in this kingdom does not involve doing what earthly kingdoms would regard as 'fitting', the implementation of grand projects, conquest of rival kingdoms, acquisition of wealth, etc. No, the most treasured service in this kingdom is the ordinary, daily task of looking after those in need—among whom the servants of the kingdom must also number themselves.

There is of course a reward for services rendered: our passage promises that Jesus' servants will be invited to share nothing less than the fullness of his kingdom. Jesus recognises and welcomes the human desire for the good, the desire to be perfect. When people ask him in the gospels how to become perfect or how to gain eternal life, he invites them to follow him and learn how to do so. A measure of our perfection will be when we can serve our brothers and sisters in some way as Christ did—for their sake and for Christ's sake, whose brothers and sisters they are—rather than for our own sake.

While there is a great reward for the sheep there is a grim punishment for the goats, the ones whose neglect has exacerbated the sorry state of the kingdom of God on earth and for which they must (in the theology of a just God) be called to account. We don't preach about hell much these days perhaps because it was overdone in days gone by. The church has never preached that anyone has been damned to hell: its brief is to preach salvation. Nevertheless both gospel passage and the church warn that eternal alienation from God is a possibility. How might one preach about hell in relation to the notion of a just and merciful God? One approach that I have explored is to use the analogy of a marriage relationship that breaks down in such a way that one partner hates the other deeply or, what is worse, both parties hate each other. In such a situation what is the more just and merciful thing to do: to oblige them to live together in a way that does violence to their own desire or to respect their freedom and let them separate?

Extras for Year A

Year 2014
Presentation of the Lord

(2 February for 4th Sunday of the Year A, 2014; Malachi 3:1–4; Hebrews 2:14–18; Luke 2:22–40).

Our reading from Luke's Gospel portrays Mary and Joseph going to the temple to do what the law required every Jewish couple who had a son as first born to do, namely, to consecrate or dedicate him to God and then to 'receive' him back from God via a sacrificial offering. In the case of Mary and Joseph who were poor people, a pair of birds sufficed. Such simple rituals, like our own, would have been a common sight in Jerusalem and no doubt, like us, the people of those days tended to take them for granted. But this ritual celebrated a massively important aspect of Israelite tradition, and, in the way Luke presents them, the arrival of Mary and Joseph with their little baby foreshadowed a massively important future for Israel and all the nations.

Why was this ritual dedication so important? Because, as the book of Exodus tells us, Pharaoh and the Egyptians refused to let God's 'first born son' (Israel) go free, dooming it to the death of slavery; hence God vowed to destroy Egypt's first born (Exodus 4:22–23) and rescue Israel. In the story of the exodus this is recounted as the tenth or last plague that afflicts Egypt while the Israelites are eating the Passover. A simple meal by slaves in the ghettoes of Egypt becomes the moment of their deliverance, their new life, but it is the moment of death for the Egyptians. From one point of view the biblical text paints a disturbing picture of God but I think our appreciation of it can be helped if we consider that this is Israel's paradigm story about overcoming the monster or evil. All cultures have versions of this kind of story, our cinemas, TV's and computer games are full of them. A common feature is that the monster (whether animal, human or alien/divine) is destroyed and the good escape the threat of death. Whatever may have happened historically in Egypt can no longer be recovered to the satisfaction of scientific analysis. The book of Exodus proclaims in dramatic story form Israel's faith that God is its deliverer from the threat of ultimate destruction. Hence it is crucial that each generation be reminded of this faith and confess it; a ritual way of doing this was to offer one's first born son to God, as well as the first born males of flocks and herds. It enabled the faithful to acknowledge their complete dependence on God and their conviction that God will deliver them at any time as God did in the exodus story—as long as one has faith.

Our reading from Luke's Gospel acknowledges the faith proclaimed by the exodus story but at the same time transforms its Old Testament horizons. The child who is presented or dedicated in the temple ritual is God's first born son in a unique way that was in due course expressed in church teaching via the doctrine of the Trinity. Moreover, Luke claims there is something much more going on here than completing a treasured ritual and then getting on with the normal routines of life, as we tend to do after our rituals. Mary and Joseph 'receive' Jesus back from God to undertake his Father's business—as the next account of him teaching in the temple while still a boy signals. Finally, while the book of Exodus is, in my view, a dramatic proclamation of faith in God as the one who overcomes the monster, Jesus sets out to overcome the real monster that threatens us all. And the monster in his 'story' is not a highly mythologised portrait of Pharaoh and Egypt but you and me, or rather the sins that afflict you and me and everyone—as Israel itself came to realise and expressed in the stories of its rebellious journey with God to the promised land (book of Numbers).

The other readings for the feast allow us to pursue this a little further. The passage from the letter to the Hebrews tells how Jesus rewrites the pervasive human view of how the monster is to be overcome—not by an act of violence against others in whom we identify sin and evil (playing the blame game), but by suffering violence without retaliating, and dying so that all might live. The reading from Malachi, the last prophetic book in the Old Testament proclaims the hope that God will eventually cleanse all evil from our lives. In the vision of this book the last, but in its view the most important, place that needs to be cleansed by God is the temple itself. Evil can enter even into temple worship, as it can enter the inner sanctum of our hearts. We may be too afraid to enter there or may reject any suggestion that evil is there but our faith teaches that Jesus is able to enter and begs us to let him do so, because it will only be for our benefit, to remake us in his image as first born sons and daughters of God.

Ss Peter and Paul, Apostles

(29 June for 13th Sunday of the Year A, 2014; Acts 12:1–11; 2 Timothy 4:6–8, 17–18; Matthew 16:13–19)

In a way it is a pity that the readings for this feast do not contain Paul's memorable account in his letter to the Galatians of his clash with Peter—how he confronted him over his duplicitous attitude to circumcision. One senses two quite different characters in conflict and, when you think about them a bit, perhaps not the kind that a modern employment agency would engage for the crucial job of getting the fledgling Christian church off the ground.

A comforting feature of the New Testament portrayals of Peter and Paul is that being a saint doesn't necessarily mean that you must be a stable, nice person. Take Peter for example. From the texts, which is about all we have, one has the impression that he was a likeable but unreliable person. When Jesus asks his disciples who they think he is, Peter comes up with the right answer. Jesus tells him that he has been chosen to make this confession by the Father and that, as a result, he will be the rock on which the church will be built. Peter is given a privileged position among the disciples but then blows it within a few verses. He remonstrates with Jesus about his prophecy of the passion and goes suddenly from being the 'rock' to 'satan'; what is worse, he subsequently denies three times the one who gave him everything. But then, according to the last chapter of the Gospel of John, he is reinstated by Jesus and given the task of shepherding the flock. Here is a fellow who was given every opportunity, blew it all, and emerges a winner nevertheless. Furthermore, there is no hint in the New Testament that the other disciples were ever jealous of Peter. They might squabble among themselves about who is the greatest but their target is never Peter. Was there something intrinsically likeable about him or was there something more? Or rather was it his awareness and acceptance that, left to his own devices, he was a complete failure and that anything that he had to offer came not from him but from Christ? Is this the real winning characteristic of Peter, the factor that makes him a great saint—and leader?

If being a stable, steady person is not equivalent to being a holy person then neither is being a nice person; just think of cranky old St Jerome for instance. How does Paul rate in the nicety stakes? As I reflect on the texts about Paul he strikes me as something like the convert who disturbs us stable cradle Catholics. A real nuisance. He comes in with his enthusiasm and enormous energy, with plans that reach well beyond the comfortable horizons that the establishment has set (to wit, the Gentile mission). He is completely dedicated to his task, at once affectionate and irascible, not suffering fools gladly and fighting with Peter, Barnabas and others. What is it about this prickly character that makes him a saint? Is it his brutal honesty and openness? Is it because Paul is always ready to give an account of his actions, to hold himself up for scrutiny as he holds others up for scrutiny? Or, rather like Peter, is it his awareness that all that he is and does comes from the grace of Christ 'who called me through his grace' and freed him from hatred of the church to become a loyal servant of the church?

A feature of the Old Testament is that it has no heroes in the romantic sense, at least not until one gets to the quite late post–exilic literature of Tobit, Esther and Daniel. The major figures of the tradition such as the ancestors Abraham, Isaac and Jacob, Moses and Aaron, David and Solomon, are all portrayed as real human beings with their strengths and weaknesses. In the main, the Old Testament has its feet too firmly fixed in the reality of human life to slip into romantic sentimentality. So also with the New Testament, if the portraits of Peter and Paul are anything to go by. They too have their strengths and weaknesses. It was God's wisdom to choose those whom the world would probably have passed over as inadequate, unreliable or too difficult. They would need to have had some counseling beforehand, done some courses to acquire people skills, etc. If these men can become the saints we celebrate today, then so can we, flawed disciples though we be.

Triumph of the Holy Cross

(14 September for 24th Sunday of the Year A, 2014; Numbers 21:4–9; Philippians 2:6–11; John 3:13–17)

The story of the fiery serpents in Numbers is a strange one; hence it exerts a certain fascination on readers who try to fathom its meaning. However, if we take a lead from its use in the Gospel of John, there is one meaning that I think we can justifiably give it—what is repulsive and death dealing from a human point of view, can with God's power and grace become life giving and something that we look up to. So the people in the Numbers story are told to look at the bronze serpent that Moses made and put on a standard. The death dealing bites of the serpents are neutralized. As well as this the story combines in a rather abrupt manner the two great ideas or theologies of God that run through the Bible: one is the just judge who is intolerant of evil and moves to root it out and punish those who perpetrate it. The law court was a crucial institution in ancient and small societies such as Israel for establishing the truth and making sure that justice was done and seen to be done. They had no universities or academies. Hence the judge became a symbol of justice and the model of how justice—righting wrong—should be administered. God above all is the righteous judge. The other is the merciful God who is all forgiving to those who call upon him. So the just judge intervenes against Israel's sin but is more than ready to show mercy to a repentant people who look up to the bronze serpent.

In the Gospel of John, Jesus draws a parallel between his passion and death and that of the bronze serpent. There is no need to labor the point that crucifixion was the most brutal and repulsive form of execution that the Romans were able to come up with. Crucifying a person and then hoisting the cross up high was supposed to be the ultimate sign of rejection and condemnation: It was a sight designed to repel onlookers and dissuade them from any association with the crucified. In a powerful reversal of how human beings see things (a theme that runs throughout the Bible), Jesus prophesies that his own crucifixion, his being lifted up on the cross, will become a sign of eternal life rather than earthly death, a sign of love and welcome rather than rejection, a sign that attracts rather than repels. How can this be so? Because in Jesus the divine and the human, the heavenly and the earthly, meet and are reconciled. This is also the thrust of the famous hymn from the letter to the Philippians. Without losing anything of his divinity (it was not something that he had to cling to in case it could be lost), Jesus enters fully into the human condition. Indeed, it is because Jesus is God that he is able to enter into the human condition in a way that no other human being can. The sign of this was his total acceptance in love of the most hateful form of death that the powers of his age could impose. The transforming power of this love—which from a human point of view looked entirely powerless—is manifest in the transformation of the cross from a hateful and deadly thing into a symbol of love and life.

The transformation of the cross wrought by Jesus transformed human lives and the symbols that express the value of human lives. The initial step was the word: the courage of Christians to proclaim their faith in Jesus' victory over sin and death and their conviction or faith that through the cross they are able to triumph over their worst fears and failings. Next came the gesture: the sign of the cross to visibly express their fellowship with their crucified and risen Lord and with one another. The third step was the visible representation of the cross for display in churches and homes. The most repulsive symbol that the Roman empire could 'create' is 'recreated' and becomes one of the most venerated and revered symbols of Christianity, a thing to look up to and place one's faith, hope and love in. The oldest surviving artistic representation of the crucifixion is apparently the one adorning a door panel of the church of Santa Sabina in Rome (4th century).

Commemoration of All the Faithful Departed

*(02 November for 31st Sunday of the Year A, 2014;
Readings from Masses for the Dead)*

'All Souls Day' as this used to be called was, for me as a boy, quite a fun day and rather satisfying. We got out of some school, marched across town to the church and vied with one another in the number of times we could duck in and out of the church and recite the required prayers to get another soul out of purgatory. It was a friendly competition with, we believed, a good outcome, however naïve our theology. Its new name, 'the Commemoration of All the Faithful Departed' looks like one of those titles where the authors have tried to pack as much meaning as they can into as few words as possible. Can we unpack it a little to get some idea of how we are meant to commemorate this important day now?

According to the dictionary, to 'commemorate' is to preserve in memory via some celebration, particularly a sacred ritual. The word therefore carries much the same meaning as when we 'remember' Jesus or commemorate him in the Eucharist. In doing this within the ritual of Christian liturgy and within the framework of our faith and its theological articulation, we believe that he is really present to those so commemorating him. It is not simply an act of memory, the recalling of something now past. Remembering in this way is a confession of Jesus' real but mysterious presence. Because the faithful departed are with God then whenever and wherever we remember the presence of God in this sacramental way, the faithful departed are present too. Even though the Eucharist is celebrated in this or that locale, it is not only a celebration by and for those of the pilgrim church but also by and for all those who have been here before us. And so we commemorate the dead in our Eucharistic prayer. This link between our daily commemoration and November 2nd is important. Otherwise the dead tend to drift out of our consciousness and our prayer. Sure, we will remember and pray for them on that one day of the year but then forget about them for the rest of the year.

When I was a boy, I thought that my prayers actually had an effect on God and that he (sic) went and opened the gates of purgatory and let another soul into heaven. Then theology got in the way with the notion of an all-knowing God who has decreed things from all eternity. I learnt that we can hang on to the notion of intercessory prayer for the dead in the sense that if the prayer we pray is for a good it is thereby part of God's eternal decree—that what is good for human beings is not withheld from them. There is also the notion that our prayer as the church is part of Christ's advocacy with the Father on behalf of all the faithful and his advocacy is, by definition, efficacious. However, I still hold onto that biblical image of God who, like a devoted parent, listens to the prayers of the children and gladly does their bidding. As Isaiah 25:8 says, God will wipe away every tear.

I like the reference to 'all the faithful' because it suggests a vast number of people, more in keeping with the sunny view of Genesis 12:1–3 than the other, more gloomy, view that only a few will be saved. It also challenges us about our selective and selfish criteria of friendship here on earth. We may like to think that we are moving towards the friendly global village but, in reality, we remain pretty choosy about our friends. Just who is included in 'all the faithful departed'? Probably a host of people who we would rather not have known or associated with if we had to share our earthly life with them: people whom we may have looked on as outsiders, the ones who were in the wrong. Yet, they are God's people and God is presumably happily bringing about their perfection (a notion of purgatory). Awareness of this may help us overcome some of our jaundiced views of others here on earth.

Finally, our commemoration speaks of the faithful as 'departed'. It is always difficult to try and describe the 'other side'; as Paul says, 'eye has not seen nor has ear heard'. We can say that the faithful have departed or 'left us' in that they are no longer present to us as we are present to ourselves, in time and space. But, as members of the church who are with God as much or more than we are, they are still very much with us. They have not left us and never will. This element of our faith enables us to look at death differently, to see that there is something binding ourselves and the faithful departed together that death cannot rupture; God's love for us. As the Song of Songs proclaims '(God's) love is stronger than death' (8:6). Psalm 63:3 puts this another way when it says of God 'your love is better than life'. Why is this so? Because God's love is the source of life; our life on earth and our life as 'the faithful departed'.

Dedication of the Lateran Basilica

(9 November for 32nd Sunday of the Year A, 2014; Ezekiel 47:1–2, 8–9; 1 Corinthians 3:9–11, 16–17; John 2:13–22)

When you walk into a massive basilica like St John Lateran's in Rome, you can't help but feel the contrast between something that has endured for hundreds of years (although this one was rebuilt several times) and the tiny ephemeral human being. One feels insignificant—is the building designed to create this impression? No, no! I can hear the Italian guide saying; it is designed to evoke the glory of God, not to demean human beings. Fair enough but this only heightens my sense of insignificance in contrast to the grandeur and glory of God. Of what worth are we? As a feast in the universal calendar, this celebration of the church of the pope as Bishop of Rome is also designed to evoke the sense of one world-wide Roman Catholic communion. At this point the choice of readings for the feast begins to make some sense and to resonate with a rich theology.

As we move through the readings, we get a sense of what a temple or church building is meant to evoke and symbolize and we realize that the Bible—as it often does—turns our impressions and expectations on their head. We are the enduring symbols of the glory of God; it is the buildings that are ephemeral and pass away. To state this is not crowing on our part: it is what the Bible claims is God's view of us, not ours. As Psalm 8 says 'When I look at the heavens . . . what are human beings that you are mindful of them? Yet you have made them little less than God'. The first reading provides an ideal starting point. Ezekiel's vision is of a wholly new and wonderful temple building but, even as he describes it in great detail, one senses that he has something more than a building in mind. Almost like the garden of Eden, the temple becomes the source of life-giving water that will sweeten and bring life to the most barren piece of water and land that an ancient Israelite could conceive of—the dead sea. The water has this creative power not because of the temple itself but because God assures Ezekiel that 'I will reside among the people of Israel forever' (43:7). The primary purpose of the temple is to symbolize the presence of God.

If one reads the passage from John's Gospel up to the point where the disciples remember the words of Psalm 69:9 (68:9), we are still within the theology of the Old Testament, of Ezekiel. The temple is meant to symbolize or evoke the presence of God ('my Father's house'); turning the temple into a market place turns it into a false symbol of God. For the sake of truth, it needs to be cleansed so that its true purpose may be seen once more. However, while there is this continuity with the Old Testament, the rest of the passage presents a new and challenging symbol of the divine presence—a new understanding of the meaning of 'temple of God'. The temple had been an enduring sign of God's presence and commitment to the people; as the Jews note, 'it has taken forty-six years to build this sanctuary'. Jesus now stands over against the temple as the definitive presence of God. Perhaps it might be more accurate to say that he stands over against the Jews' perception of the temple and its purpose. If they could stand inside the cleansed temple and accept that this is how it should be then, John's Gospel implies, they should be able to see that Jesus is the fulfillment of all that the temple symbolises.

Jesus, a human being who can and will be killed (destroyed) is the enduring sign of God in creation. But the purpose of the incarnation is not just to draw attention to Jesus as the temple of God that has been 'erected' in our midst. Paul tells his Corinthian Christians that they too are part of this temple. Jesus is the foundation stone of God's building of which they are all a part. This 'building' made up of human beings is a continual work in progress. Becoming one of the 'stones' is not the end of the matter, far from it. As Paul writes, everyone needs to work carefully on this building that will grow as long as Jesus remains the sure foundation stone. This 'temple' of human beings is the most enduring thing in creation. Our world will pass away and all that we have built on it, but the communion of saints called church will never pass away. As a final thought for this feast, one might add that if we human beings were able to be to one another (and to creation) what God made and meant us to be—the image and likeness of God—then there would be no need for temples and churches. In a way, they are a sign of our own inadequacy and failure as human beings.

Year 2017
Transfiguration

---

*(06 August for 18th Sunday of the Year A; Daniel 7:9–10, 13–14;
2 Peter 1:16–19; Matthew 17:1–9)*

When you are continually disappointed despite your best efforts, or when people keep telling you that you are a nobody and a failure, it can be hard to keep your spirits up, to look beyond the ever decreasing world in which you live. The amazing thing about a book like Daniel (a *nom–de–plume* of an anonymous author) is that although it was written at a time of great trial and suffering for the Jewish people it nevertheless confidently asserts the ultimate triumph of God's purpose, a purpose that will transform all nations, even those that oppress Israel. Here is an author who seeks to enshrine the message of the great prophets via a series of visions (a recognition perhaps that the prophetic word is at present silent) apparently without the slightest personal evidence to confirm that their prophecies are being realized. Something akin to the Carmelite spirituality of the dark night of the soul.

The book of Daniel proclaims its conviction that the prophecies of God's triumph over sin and evil will come true, the Christian claim is that the life and teachings of Jesus reveal how this takes place. The transfiguration can be seen as a kind of down payment on it, or a glimpse of it. Somewhat like the visions in Daniel it takes place at a fraught stage in Matthew's Gospel when Jesus begins to tell his disciples about his coming death and resurrection. Moreover, it is almost a private occasion with only three of the disciples with Jesus on the mountain, who are forbidden by him to tell anyone about the transfiguration until after 'the son of man has risen from the dead'. The implication is that otherwise people will not understand it; even the three disciples will need to take special care that they do not misunderstand it when Jesus enters his passion and death. Jesus and the disciples then rejoin the others at the foot of the mountain and are immediately embroiled in a dispute about an exorcism. Jesus casts out the demon and then reiterates the prophecy about his death and resurrection.

The transfiguration is clearly linked to Jesus' death and resurrection via these repeated references or prophecies, something that the Lucan version makes explicit by the way it presents Moses and Elijah speaking with Jesus about 'his passing which he was to accomplish in Jerusalem' (Lk 9:31). For us who read the Gospel in the light of Jesus' death and resurrection, this means that Jesus' suffering and death on the cross is as much a revelation of his unique status as God's beloved son as the transfiguration itself. What happens at the place/mountain of crucifixion may not look like it but to those enabled to 'see' it is as much a transfiguration of Jesus as what happens on the mountain of transfiguration. Both reveal the fulfillment of the prophecies and thereby assure us that God's plan of salvation is coming to fruition. What will enable one to 'see' and understand this? Listening, as the voice from the cloud says on the mountain of transfiguration, to the words of 'my beloved son'. The importance of this, not only for the disciples in the gospel but for disciples of any generation, is underscored by the reading from the second letter of Peter. The writer, whether Peter or a disciple writing in his name, appeals to the transfiguration to assure readers that they can rely on the prophetic word as a lamp that will light their way. Why is this so? Because the prophetic word, cast in visionary form in the book of Daniel, was confirmed by nothing less than the words and actions of Jesus.

Of course we will fail like the disciples in the gospel. But Jesus is merciful and welcoming despite our failures. This is shown by the way he invites Peter to accompany him up the mountain of transfiguration even though Peter has rebuked him about his prophecy that he must go to Jerusalem and die, and is dubbed 'Satan' by Jesus for his pains. It is also shown by the way the resurrected Jesus instructs the women to tell his failed and frightened disciples to go to Galilee where they will meet him on the mountain (28:16). Matthew does not specify whether this is the mountain of the transfiguration or of the beatitudes. Given the context of the resurrection, one may presume it is the former because it is there that the eleven disciples see the risen Lord in his glory and worship him, another transfiguration scene as it were. There too they receive Jesus' commission to make disciples of all nations, not by turning them into Jews, Persians, Greeks or Romans but by baptizing them in the name of the Father and of the Son and of the Holy Spirit. A new identity that transcends the old divisions and creates a new family of humanity. The promises of the great prophets about the gathering of the nations, the visions of the seer in the book of Daniel are being fulfilled, even though we may at times—like the author of Daniel—lack evidence that it is advancing in our day.

Suggested For Further Reading

Alter, Robert. *The Art of Biblical Narrative* (New York: Basic Books, 1981).

Alter, Robert. *The Art of Biblical Poetry* (New York: Basic Books, 1985).

Bassler, Jouette M. *Navigating Paul: An Introduction to Key Theological Concepts* (Louisville: Westminster John Knox, 2007).

Birch, Bruce C (and others). *A Theological Introduction to the Old Testament* (Nashville: Abingdon, 2005).

Brueggemann, Walter J. *An Introduction to the Old Testament: The Canon and Christian Imagination* (Louisville: Westminster John Knox, 2003).

Byrne, Brendan J. *The Hospitality of God: A Reading of Luke's Gospel* (Collegeville: Liturgical Press, 2000).

Byrne, Brendan J. *Lifting the Burden: Reading Matthew's Gospel in the Church Today* (Collegeville: Liturgical Press, 2004).

Bryne, Brendan J. *A Costly Freedom: A Theological Reading of Mark's Gospel* (Collegeville: Liturgical Press, 2008).

Campbell, Antony F. *The Whisper of Spirit. A Believable God Today* (Grand Rapids: Eerdmans, 2008).

Campbell, Antony F. *God and Bible: Exploring Stories from Genesis to Job* (New York/Mahwah: Paulist, 2008).

Crenshaw, James L. *Old Testament Wisdom: An Introduction* (Louisville: Westminster John Knox, 1998

Fretheim, Terence E. *The Pentateuch* (Nashville: Abingdon Press, 1996).

Horrell, David G. *An Introduction to the Study of Paul.* London: T & T Clark, 2006

Johnson, Luke Timothy *The Writings of the New Testament: An Interpretation* (Minneapolis: Fortress, 2010).

Moloney, Francis J. *The Gospel of John* (Collegeville: Liturgical Press, 1998).

Moloney, Francis, J. *The Living Voice of the Gospels.* Peabody: Hendrickson, 2006

Sweeney, Marvin A. *The Prophetic Literature* (Nashville: Abingdon, 2005).

Articles in Dictionaries such as *The Anchor Bible Dictionary* and *The New Interpreters Dictionary of the Bible.* Both are available in most theological libraries.

Biblical Index

The page numbers with an 'f' indicate a particular Sunday's Readings, while those with no 'f' are references to incidental Scripture passages

Old Testament

Genesis
1:1 – 2:2, 55f
1:1, 55f
1:2, 75
1:26-31, 55f
1:26, 6, 79
2 – 11, 36
2, 42
2:7-9, 31f
3:1-7, 31f
6:1-4, 25
12, 36, 101
12:1-4, 35f
12:1-3, 182
15, 102
16, 102
20, 101
22, 102
22:1-18, 55
38, 19

Exodus
4:22-23, 175
12:5, 169
12:1-18, 49f
12:11-14, 49f
14:15 – 15:1, 55f
17:3-7, 39f
19:2-6, 103f
21:24, 95

22:20-26, 155f
24, 103
25:8, 25
34, 35
34:4-6, 79f
34:8-9, 79f

Leviticus
17 – 26, 96
19:1-2, 95f
19:17-18, 95f
19:18, 155

Numbers
6:22-27, 25f
11:4-6, 39
21:4-9, 179f

Deuteronomy
4:6, 128
6:5, 155
7, 129
8:2-3, 81f
8:14-16, 81f
11:18, 99f
11:26-28, 99f
19:1-2,
19:17, 18, 95
19:17-26, 96

19:18, 134, 155
23, 19

Joshua
2, 19

Judges
13:5, 23
13:7, 23

1 Kings
3 – 8, 59
3:5-7, 119f
3:7-12, 119f
19:9, 125f
19:11-13, 125f

2 Kings
2, 14
4, 14
4:8-11, 109f
4:14-16, 109f
16:2-4, 15
21, 20

Wisdom
6:12-16, 163f
12:13, 117f
12:16-19, 117f

Psalms
22, 46
23, 63
73, 164
117, 148
118, 147
146:6-7, 87f
146:8-9a, 87f
146:9b-10, 87f

Proverbs
9, 166
10:1 – 31:9, 167

31:10-13, 165f
31:19-20, 165f
31:30-31, 165f

1 Samuel
16:1, 41f
16:10-13, 41f

Sirach
3:2-6, 23f
15:15-20, 93f
27:30 – 28:7, 135f

Isaiah
2:1-5, 9f
2:1-4, 147
5:1-7, 147f
6:9-10, 114
7:10-14, 15f
8:23 – 9:31, 85f
9:1-7, 17f
11:1-10, 11f
22:15, 129f
22:19-23, 129f
25:6-10, 151f
26:8, 182
35:1-6, 13f
35:10, 13f
40 – 55, 113
40:27-31, 113
42:1-4, 29f, 83
42:6-7a, 29f
45:1, 153f
45:4-6, 153f
49:3, 83f
49:5-6, 83f
49:14-15, 97f
50:4-9, 83
50:4-7, 45f
52:7-10, 19f
52:13 – 53:12, 51f, 83
53:1-7, 84
54:5-14, 55f

55:1-3, 123f
55:6-9, 139f
55:1-11, 55f
55:1-3, 123f
55:10-11, 113f
56, 127
56:1, 127f
56:6-7, 127f
58:7-10, 91f
60:1-6, 27f
62:1-5, 19f
62:11-12, 19f

Jeremiah
20:7-9, 131f
20:10-13, 105f
26:1, 107
31:15, 23
31:29, 143

Baruch
3:9-15, 55f
3: 32 – 4:4, 55f

Ezekiel
18:25-28, 143f
33:7-9, 133f

34:11-12, 169f
34:15-17, 169f
37:12-14, 43f
36:16-17a, 55f
36:18-28, 55f
47:1-2, 185f
47:8-9, 185f

Daniel
7:9-10, 187f
7:13-14, 187f

Hosea
6:3-6, 101f

Zephaniah
2:3, 87f
3:12-13, 87f

Zechariah
9:9-10, 111f

Malachi
1:14 – 2:2, 159f
2:8-10, 159f
3:1-4, 175f

New Testament

Matthew
1:1-25, 19f
1:18-25, 19f
1:18-25, 15f
1:23, 23
2:1-12, 27f
2:6, 23
2:15, 23
2:18, 23
2:13-15, 23f
2:19-23, 23f
2:23, 23
3:1-12, 11f
3:2, 85, 87
3:13-17, 29f
4:1-11, 31f
4:12-23, 85f
4:12-17, 85f
4:17, 87
5:1-12, 87f
5:16, 99
5:17-31, 93f
5:32, 99
5:38-48, 95f
7:21-27, 99f
9:9-13, 101f
9:36 – 10:8, 103f
10:1-42, 106
10:1-15, 106
10:1-10, 63f
10:26-33, 105f
10:26, 106
10:28, 106
10:31, 106
10:34-42, 106
10:37-42, 109f
11:2-11, 13f
11:25-30, 111f
12, 23
12:46-50, 24
13:1-23, 113f

13:1-9 113f
13:24-43, 117f
13:24-30, 117f
13:44-52, 119f
13:44-46, 119f
14:13-21, 123f
14:22-33, 125f
15:21-28, 127f
16:13-20, 129f
16:13-19, 177f
16:21-27, 131f
17:1-9, 35f, 187f
18:15-20, 133f
18:21-35, 135f
20:1-16, 139f
21:28-32, 143f
21:33-43, 147f
22:1-14, 151f
22:1-10, 151f
22:15-21, 153f
22:34-40, 155f
23:1-12, 159f
24:37-44, 9f
25, 165
25:1-13, 163f
24:14-30, 165f
25:14-15, 165f
25:19-20, 165f
25:31-46, 169f
26:14 – 27:66, 45
27:11-59, 45
28:1-10, 55f
28:16-20, 73f

Luke
2:1-14, 17f
2:15-20, 19f
2:16-21, 25f
2:22-40, 175f
9:31, 188

24:13-35, 61f
29:37, 61

John
1:1-18, 19f
1:19 – 12:50, 43
1:29-34, 83f
2 – 12, 41
2:13-22, 185f
3:13-17, 179f
3:16-18, 79f
4:5-42, 39f
4:5-15, 39f
4:19-26, 39f
4:39, 39f
4:40-42, 39f
6:51-58, 81f
8:44, 64
9:1-41, 41f
9:1, 41f
9:6-9, 41f
9:13-17, 41f
9:34-38, 41f
10:1-10, 63f
10:11-16, 63
10:11-18, 43
11:1-45, 43f
11:3-7, 43f
11:17, 43f
11:20-27, 43f
11:33-45, 43f
12, 49
12:32, 43
13:1 – 20:31, 43
13:1-15, 49f
14:1-12, 67f, 71
14: 15-21, 71f
18:1 – 19:42, 51f
20:19-31, 59f
20:19-23, 75f

Acts of the Apostles
1:1-11, 73f
2:1-11, 75f
2:42-47, 59f
2:14, 61f, 63f
2:36-41, 63f
2:22-28, 61f
6:1-17, 67f
8:5-8, 71f
8:14-17, 71f
10:34-38, 29f
12:1-11, 177f
13:16-17, 19f
13:22-25, 19f

Romans
1:1-7, 15f
3:21-25, 99f
3:28, 99f
4:18-25, 101f
5:1-2, 39f
5:5-8, 39f
5:6-11, 103f
5:12-19, 31f
5:12, 31f
5:12-15, 105f
5:17-19, 31f
6:3-4, 109f
6:8-11, 109f
8:8-11, 43f
8:9, 111f
8:11-13, 111f
8:18-23, 113f
8:23-27, 126
8:26-27, 117f
8:28-30, 119f
8:35, 123f
8:37-39, 123f
9:1-5, 125f
11:13-15, 127f
11:29-32, 127f
11:33-36, 129f
12:1-2, 131f

13:8-10, 133f
14:7-9, 135f
13:11-14, 9f
15:4-9, 11f

1 Corinthians
1:1-3, 83f
1:10-13, 83f
1:17, 83f
1:26-31, 87f
2:1-5, 91f
2:6-10, 93f
3:16-23, 95f
4:1-5, 97f
10:16-17, 81f
11:23-26, 49f
12:3-7, 75f
12:12-13, 75f

1 Corinthians
1:10-13, 85f
1:17, 85f
3:9-11, 185f
3:16-17, 185f
15:20-26, 169f
15:28, 169f

2 Corinthians
13:11-13, 79f

Galatians
4:4-7, 25f

Ephesians
1:17-23, 73f
3:2-3, 27f
3:5-6, 27f
5:8-14, 41f

Philippians
1:20-24, 139f
1:27, 139f
2:1-11, 143f

2:6-11, 45f, 179f
4:6-9, 147f
4:12-14, 151f
4:19-20, 151f

Colossians
3:12-21, 23f

1 Thessalonians
1:1-5, 153f
1:5-10, 155f
2:7-9, 159f
2:13, 159f
4:13-18, 163f
5:1-6, 165f

2 Timothy
1:8-10, 35f
4:6-8, 177f
4:17-18, 177f

Titus
2:11-14, 17f

Hebrews
1:1-6, 19f
2:14-18, 175f
4:14-16, 51f
5:7-9, 51f

James
5:7-10, 13f

1 Peter
1:3-9, 59f
1:17-21, 61f
2:4-9, 67f
2:20-25, 63f
3:15-18, 71f

2 Peter
1:16-19, 187
28:16, 188

Subject Index

Aaron,	24, 25, 178		130, 147, 148,
Ananias,	9		154, 164, 175, 176,
angel,	16, 17, 18, 20, 29,		179, 187
	44, 56, 57,	faith,	3, 4, 5, 10, 13, 14,
	61, 62, 102, 120		15, 19, 26, 35,
crucifixion, the,	47, 52, 55, 56, 57,		41, 42, 51, 57, 59,
	179, 180, 188		60, 62, 71, 72, 73,
David,	15, 16, 19, 20, 23,		74, 80, 81, 100,
	153, 178		101, 102, 105, 106,
disciple,	13, 14, 16, 20, 23,		107, 113, 117, 124,
	24, 26, 30, 35, 36,		125, 128, 129, 130,
	40, 41, 42, 44, 45,		133, 135, 141, 153,
	46, 49, 50, 56, 57,		159, 163, 164, 165
	61, 62, 63, 64, 68,		166, 176, 180, 181,
	72, 73, 74, 75, 86,		182, 183
	87, 88, 92, 96, 100,	fear,	5, 10, 15, 16, 18,
	104, 106, 110,112,		27,28,36, 46, 55, 56,
	114,119,120,124,		57, 60, 61, 64, 72,
	126, 130, 131, 132,		73, 97, 102, 106,
	134, 139, 141,145,		111, 126, 132, 166,
	148, 151, 163, 164,		180
	170,177, 178, 186,	forgiveness,	2, 113, 135, 136
	187, 188	grace,	5, 16, 26, 32, 42,
Easter,	44, 55, 59, 61, 63,		52, 55, 57,
	64, 67, 71, 169		71, 80, 84, 86, 89,
Elijah,	14, 35, 36, 125, 188		93, 96, 100,
Elisha,	41, 110, 125		109, 120, 214, 129,
Emmaus,	61, 62		136, 145, 160, 170,
eucharist, the,	50, 62, 81, 82, 181		178, 179
evil,	2, 4, 5, 45, 50, 51,	hope,	10, 12, 31, 57, 59,
	80, 82, 106, 112,		60, 61, 67,
	114, 115, 117, 118,		71, 72, 73, 81,

	101, 102, 105, 106, 125, 126, 128, 135, 147, 176, 180	prophecy,	13, 14, 35, 36, 45, 46, 97, 115, 124, 140, 147, 153, 177, 188
image and likeness,	6, 14, 21, 50, 51, 52, 56, 57, 63, 74, 79, 80, 130, 154, 186	prophet,	3, 5, 13, 14, 24, 36, 40, 41, 42, 46, 62, 80, 92, 93, 95, 97, 101, 107, 109, 110,
joy,	27, 37, 40, 56, 57, 60, 72, 80, 81, 87 88, 98, 104, 114, 123, 124, 126, 136, 160, 164		111, 113, 125, 126, 127, 132, 133, 143, 147, 151, 160, 176, 187, 188, 189
Lazarus,	43, 44, 49	resurrection, the,	5, 43, 44, 51, 56, 57, 59, 60, 61, 62, 73,
love,	4, 5, 12, 16, 20, 28, 30, 32, 36,		74, 124, 140, 144, 164, 167, 188
	42, 43, 44, 49, 50, 51, 52, 53, 57,	righteousness,	29, 53, 88, 94, 96, 98, 134, 147, 148
	59, 60, 71, 72, 80, 82, 88, 96, 100, 101, 102, 103, 104, 105,106, 110, 120, 123, 129, 130	salvation,	4, 13, 16, 28, 46, 50, 60, 64, 68, 72, 73, 83, 86, 96, 112, 166, 170, 188
	134,135, 140, 141, 148, 152, 155, 156, 157, 160,164, 180, 182, 183, 188	Sapphira, servant,	59 28, 30, 45, 46, 83, 98, 110, 136, 137, 144, 148, 151, 152, 160, 165, 166, 170,
mercy,	4, 5,6, 50, 126, 128, 135, 136, 179	sign,	178 15, 16, 29, 36, 41, 42, 43, 44, 47, 49, 50,
messiah,	11, 40, 153		53, 57, 62, 73, 74, 80,
metaphor,	64, 67, 68, 69, 97, 98, 130, 164		82, 87, 102, 111, 112,130, 132, 144,
Moses,	23, 24, 25, 35, 36, 39, 79, 80, 87, 93 100, 103, 128, 153, 178, 179, 188	sin,	152, 156, 164, 166, 179, 180, 186 2, 3, 4, 5, 9, , 12, 13, 14, 16, 18, 20, 21, 24,
passion, the,	43, 44, 45, 46, 56, 73, 104, 177, 179, 187		25, 27, 28, 29, 30, 31, 32, 36, 37, 39, 40, 42, 43, 44, 47, 49, 51, 52,
priest,	14, 24, 45, 46, 103, 133, 144, 148, 160		53, 59, 61, 62, 63, 64, 65, 72, 75, 76, 80, 81, 83, 84, 86, 87,

	88, 89, 95, 100, 102, 104, 105, 107, 112, 113, 114, 117, 119, 120, 125, 127, 128, 129, 130, 132, 135, 136, 140, 143, 154, 159, 160, 164, 165, 166, 176, 179, 187, 188
Solomon,	20, 59, 120, 121, 178
Spirit, the Holy,	5, 29, 30, 64, 74, 75, 76, 79, 80, 82, 83, 98, 112, 118, 124, 154, 188
suffering,	46, 52, 56, 57, 62, 83, 99, 104, 152, 176, 178, 188
tomb, the	30, 44, 47, 56
spiritual,	67, 68, 81, 112
Torah Law, the,	24, 25, 32, 35, 36, 39, 80, 93, 99, 100, 106, 128, 131, 133, 134, 136, 144, 155, 156
worship,	1, 6, 40, 67, 68, 101, 156, 176, 188

Milton Keynes UK
Ingram Content Group UK Ltd.
UKHW012126040923
428043UK00006B/851